TALK TO ME IN KOREAN
LEVEL 3

Expand Your Knowledge of Korean
by Learning Irregularities, Linking Verbs, Politeness Levels,
and Much More

This book is based on a series of published lessons,
divided into ten levels, which are currently available
at https://talktomeinkorean.com.

Talk To Me In Korean - Level 3

1판 1쇄 • 1st edition published		2015. 12. 7.
1판 17쇄 • 17th edition published		2024. 6. 24.

지은이 • Written by		Talk To Me In Korean
책임편집 • Edited by		선경화 Kyung-hwa Sun, 스테파니 베이츠 Stephanie Bates
디자인 • Designed by		선윤아 Yoona Sun
삽화 • Illustrations by		김경해 Kyounghae Kim
녹음 • Voice Recordings by		선현우 Hyunwoo Sun, 최경은 Kyeong-eun Choi
펴낸곳 • Published by		롱테일북스 Longtail Books
펴낸이 • Publisher		이수영 Su Young Lee
편집 • Copy-edited by		김보경 Florence Kim
주소 • Address		04033 서울특별시 마포구 양화로 113, 3층(서교동, 순흥빌딩)
		3rd Floor, 113 Yanghwa-ro, Mapo-gu, Seoul, KOREA
이메일 • E-mail		TTMIK@longtailbooks.co.kr
ISBN		979-11-86701-09-6 14710

*이 교재의 내용을 사전 허가 없이 전재하거나 복제할 경우 법적인 제재를 받게 됨을 알려 드립니다.

*잘못된 책은 구입하신 서점이나 본사에서 교환해 드립니다.

*정가는 표지에 표시되어 있습니다.

TTMIK - TALK TO ME IN KOREAN

MESSAGE
FROM
THE AUTHOR

안녕하세요, and welcome to Level 3! This book series (as with the majority of our learning material) is designed to help you learn Korean on your own in case you do not have the opportunity to attend classroom lessons. Study anywhere at any time with this book, and if you have any questions, please contact us and we will do our best to help you.

When learning a new language, especially if embarking on a self-study journey, it is very important to find a variety of ways to help improve your listening, speaking, reading, and writing skills. We strongly recommend seeking out other resources to help with your language study. There is a workbook available to accompany this book in addition to free MP3 audio files to download and take with you wherever you go. We, and a community of Korean learners just like you, are always available on your favorite social media network to help you practice.

The most important thing about learning a new language is to have fun doing it and never be afraid of making mistakes! Thank you for giving us your support and for studying with Talk To Me In Korean. Good luck with your studies, and have fun with Level 3!

TABLE OF CONTENTS

LESSON 1

Too much, Very

너무

Track 01

Welcome to Talk To Me In Korean Level 3, and congratulations on making it through the first two levels of the curriculum! In Level 3, you will build upon what you have previously learned through Levels 1 and 2.

In this lesson, you will learn how to use 너무. This word is used every day in Korean with two different meanings: the original dictionary meaning and the more colloquial meaning.

Basic meaning:

너무 = too (much), excessively

The dictionary meaning of 너무 is "too much" or "excessively".

Sample Sentences

너무 커요.

= It is too big.

너무 비싸요.

= It is too expensive.

너무 빨라요.

= It is too fast.

너무 어려워요.

= It is too difficult.

Track 01

너무 시끄러워요.

= It is too noisy.

소연 씨 너무 커요.

= Soyeon, you are too tall.

이거 너무 비싸요.

= This is too expensive.

말이 너무 빨라요.

= (Someone) speaks too fast.

한국어 너무 어려워요.

= The Korean language is too difficult.

9

여기 너무 시끄러워요.

= It is too noisy here.

Colloquial usage

너무 = very, quite (sometimes also used in a shortened form as 넘, but only in very casual language.)

Although the basic meaning of the word 너무 is "too much" or "excessively", in colloquial Korean, it also has the meaning of "very", "quite", or "really".

Sample Sentences

Track 01

너무 맛있어요.

= It is really tasty.

너무 좋아요.

= It is really good.

= I am really happy about it.

너무 잘했어요.

= It is really well done.

= You did such a good job.

너무 멋있어요.

= It is really cool.

= It looks awesome.

이 피자 너무 맛있어요.

= This pizza is really tasty.

이거 너무 좋아요.

= I really like this.

석진 씨, 너무 잘했어요.

= Seokjin, you did a really great job.

저 모델 너무 멋있어요!

= That model is really cool!

In the past, 너무 was used only in negative sentences or contexts, but it has gradually become acceptable to use in positive contexts as well. Now, most people use 너무 both ways.

Track 01

Ex)

너무 더워요.

= It is too hot.

= It is very hot.

너무 졸려요.

= I am too sleepy.

= I am very sleepy.

너무 바빠요.

= I am too busy.

= I am very busy.

11

너무 is usually combined with adjectives, but it can also be used with verbs as well.

Ex)

너무 보고 싶어요.

= I miss you/him/her/them so much.

Track 01

12

Sample Dialogue

Track
02

A: 너무 배고파요.

B: 점심 안 먹었어요?

A: 네, 아직 안 먹었어요.

B: 얼른 먹어요.

A: *I am really hungry.*

B: *Have you not had lunch yet?*

A: *No, I haven't eaten yet.*

B: *Go ahead and eat.*

by Learning Irregularities, Linking Verbs, Politeness Levels, and Much More

✏ Exercises for Lesson 1

1. What is the Korean word which means "too much" or "excessively"?

( )

2. How do you write "very" or "quite" in colloquial Korean?

( )

3. Write "it's too fast" in Korean.

( )

4. How is "it's really tasty" said in Korean?

( )

5. In Korean, write "I'm too sleepy."

( )

Check the answers on **p.196**

LESSON **2**

Linking Verbs

-고

Just speaking in simple sentences can get your point across, but would not it be nice to shorten what you are saying and connect sentences together while still being able to express exactly what you want?

One way to accomplish this is by making compound nouns which are also known as "noun phrases" or "nominal phrases". Of course there are many different ways to make compound nouns depending on what is to be said, but in this lesson, you will learn how the verb ending -고 is used.

-고

So what exactly does -고 do? Do you remember the conjunction 그리고? Yes, 그리고 means "and" or "and then" in Korean, so when using -고 after a verb stem, it has the same meaning as 그리고. By using the verb ending -고 rather than ending the sentence with just one verb and then starting the next one with 그리고, you can save a lot of time and make your sentence structures more practical.

이 책은 재미있어요. 그리고 이 책은 싸요.

= This book is interesting. And this book is cheap.

Since you are talking about the same subject in the second sentence, you can just omit the second "이 책은".

→ 이 책은 재미있어요. 그리고 싸요.

= This book is interesting. And (it is) cheap.

Combine the two sentences together to make it shorter while still getting the point across.

Track 03

→ 이 책은 재미있고 싸요.

= This book is interesting and cheap.

> ### Conjugation
>
> Verb stem + **-고** + another verb

Ex)
이 책은 재미있고, 싸고, 좋아요.

= This book is interesting, cheap, and good.

* When making a compound sentence in English using the conjunction "and" to connect smaller sentences, the tenses of the verbs need to agree. However, in Korean, it is not absolutely necessary to have verb tenses match, and sometimes it sounds unnatural to try to use the same tenses for every verb - especially the future tense and the past tense. Most

16

native Korean speakers just use the past tense or the future tense with only the final verb. ** Also, it is worth noting that -고 can sometimes sound like "구" in casual, spoken Korean - particularly amongst younger women. Do not get confused however, even if your friend might say it with a "구" sound, it is still written and referred to as -고.

Past tense example

어제 친구를 만났어요.

= I met a friend yesterday.

그리고 영화를 봤어요.

= And I saw a movie.

Let's put the two sentences above together.

Track 03

어제 친구를 만났어요. 그리고 영화를 봤어요.
→ 어제 친구를 만났고, 영화를 봤어요.

= I met a friend yesterday and saw a movie.

Furthermore, "어제 친구를 만나고, 영화를 봤어요" with "만나고" in present tense can also be said.

Future tense example

내일 영화를 볼 거예요.

= I will watch a movie tomorrow.

서점에 갈 거예요.

= I will go to a bookstore.

내일 영화를 볼 거예요. 그리고 서점에 갈 거예요.

→ 내일 영화를 볼 거고, 서점에 갈 거예요.

= Tomorrow, I will watch a movie, and go to a bookstore.

"내일 영화를 보고, 서점에 갈 거예요" can also be said.

Since 그리고 (or in this case, -고) has the meaning of "and after that" or "and then", using -고 is a good way of talking about things that happened or will happen in a sequence.

Track 03

Sample Sentences

내일은 친구 만나고, 서점에 갈 거예요.

= As for tomorrow, I am going to meet a friend and go to a bookstore.

책 읽고, 공부하고, 운동했어요.

= I read a book, studied, and did some exercise.

9월에는 한국에 가고, 10월에는 일본에 갈 거예요.

= I will go to Korea in September, and I will go to Japan in October.

커피 마시고, 도넛 먹고, 케이크 먹고, 우유 마셨어요. 배불러요.

= I drank some coffee, ate a donut, ate some cake, and drank some milk. I am full.

Sample Dialogue

A: 어제 영화 보고 뭐 했어요?

B: 어제 영화 보고 밥 먹었어요.

A: 밥 먹고 집에 갔어요?

B: 네.

A: *What did you do after you watched the movie
yesterday?*

B: *I ate after I watched the movie yesterday.*

A: *Did you go home after you ate?*

B: *Yes.*

by Learning Irregularities, Linking Verbs, Politeness Levels, and Much More

🖊 Exercises for Lesson 2

Check the answers on **p.196**

1. Write "I met a friend yesterday, and saw a movie" in Korean.

    * I met a friend yesterday. = 어제 친구를 만났어요.

    * And I saw a movie. = 그리고 영화를 봤어요.

    (   )

2. In Korean, write "Tomorrow, I will watch a movie, and go shopping."

    * I will watch a movie tomorrow. = 내일 영화를 볼 거예요.

    * I will go shopping. = 쇼핑하러 갈 거예요.

    (   )

3. How do you say "As for tomorrow, I'm going to meet a friend and go to a bookstore"?

    * To meet = 만나다

내일은 친구 (   ) 서점에 갈 거예요.

4. How would you write "After I got home yesterday, I ate and slept"?

    * To eat = 먹다

어제 집에 가서 (   ) 잤어요.

5. Write "I read a book, studied, and did some exercise" in Korean.

    * To read = 읽다   * To study = 공부하다   * To do exercise = 운동하다

    (   )

LESSON 3

In front of, Behind, Next to, On top of, Under

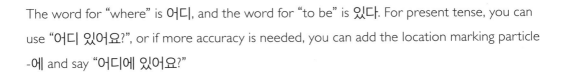

앞에, 뒤에, 옆에, 위에, 밑에

In this lesson, you will learn how to describe the relative location of things and people.

Track
05

The word for "where" is 어디, and the word for "to be" is 있다. For present tense, you can use "어디 있어요?", or if more accuracy is needed, you can add the location marking particle -에 and say "어디에 있어요?"

어디 있어요?

= 어디에 있어요?

= Where is it? / Where are you? / Where are they?

어디 있었어요?

= 어디에 있었어요?

= Where were you? / Where have you been?

21

어디 있을 거예요?

= 어디에 있을 거예요?

= Where will you be? / Where are you going to be?

In order to give a response to this question, use one of the following five one-syllable words:

앞 = front

뒤 = back

옆 = side

위 = top

밑 = bottom

Track
05

To use these syllables with other words, you add -에: the location marking particle.

앞에 = in front of

뒤에 = behind

옆에 = beside, next to

위에 = over, on top of

밑에 = under, below

In English, these words come BEFORE the words which they modify, but in Korean, they come AFTER the words.

Ex)

자동차 = car, automobile

자동차 앞에 = in front of the car

자동차 뒤에 = behind the car

22

자동차 옆에 = beside the car; next to the car

자동차 위에 = on the car; on top of the car

자동차 밑에 = under the car

Combined with 있다:

자동차 앞에 있어요. = It is in front of the car.

자동차 뒤에 있어요. = It is behind the car.

자동차 옆에 있어요. = It is next to the car.

자동차 위에 있어요. = It is on top of the car.

자동차 밑에 있어요. = It is under the car.

In Level 1, Lesson 18, it was mentioned that -에 is only used with the status of a person or an object. When expressing actions and behaviors which are actively happening, use -에서.

Track 05

Ex)

Q: 친구를 어디에서 만날 거예요?

 = Where are you going to meet (your) friends?

A: 은행 앞에서 만날 거예요.

 = I am going to meet (them) in front of the bank.   * 은행 = bank

A: 은행 뒤에서 만날 거예요.

 = I am going to meet (them) behind the bank.

A: 은행 옆에서 만날 거예요.

 = I am going to meet (them) beside the bank.

Sample Sentences

소파 위에서 자고 있어요.

= I am sleeping on the sofa.

나무 밑에서 책을 읽고 있어요.

= I am reading a book under the tree.

나무 뒤에 숨어 있었어요.

= I have been hiding behind the tree.

문 앞에서 통화하고 있었어요.

= I was talking on the phone in front of the door.

Track
05

Sample Dialogue

A: 머리에 뭐 묻었어요.

B: 여기요?

A: 아니요. 그 옆에요. 좀 더 밑에요.

A: *There is something in your hair.*

B: *Here?*

A: *No. Next to it. A little more below that.*

by Learning Irregularities, Linking Verbs, Politeness Levels, and Much More

✏ *Exercises for Lesson* **3**

Match the Korean word to its English equivalent.

1. 앞   a. front

2. 위   b. back

3. 밑   c. side

4. 뒤   d. top

5. 옆   e. bottom

6. Fill in the blank with a word which best completes the Korean sentence.

= 소파 (   ) 자고 있어요.

(I am sleeping on the sofa.)

Expand Your Knowledge of Korean

LESSON 4

Shall we…?, I wonder…

-(으)ㄹ까요?

Track 07

The sentence structure you will learn in this lesson is really convenient. Not only can -(으)ㄹ까요? be used to ask someone a question such as "Do you want to do this with me?", but it can also be used to say "I wonder what the weather will be like tomorrow" or "Will it be expensive to go to Korea?" As you can see, in English, you have to use many different words and expressions to say these sentences, but thanks to -(으)ㄹ까요? you can say these things and much more in Korean very easily!

-(으)ㄹ까요?

Usage 1: Asking oneself a question or showing doubt about something

Ex)

"I wonder what is in this bag?"

"Will he be alright?"

27

"Will it be hot tomorrow?"

"What will she say?"

Usage 2: Raising a question and attracting attention of others

Ex)

"Why did this happen? What do you think, everyone?"

"What do you think life is?"

Usage 3: Suggesting doing something together

Track 07

Ex)

"What shall we do now?"

"Shall we go to the movies?"

"Do you want me to help you?"

Q : How do you know which of these meanings it takes?

A : It is fairly clear and easy to see which meaning it takes when looking at the context.

Conjugation

Verb stems ending with a consonant + -을까요?

Verb stems ending with a vowel + -ㄹ까요?

(Exception) Verb stems ending with ㄹ + -까요?

Ex)

먹다 (to eat) becomes 먹을까요?

보다 (to see) becomes 볼까요?

팔다 (to sell) becomes 팔까요?

시작하다 (to start) becomes 시작할까요?

공부하다 (to study) becomes 공부할까요?

달리다 (to run) becomes 달릴까요?

놀다 (to play) becomes 놀까요?

살다 (to live) becomes 살까요?

Track 07

By using -ㄹ까요? or -을까요? it is showing curiosity or uncertainty. For example, in usage #1, when asking yourself a question and showing doubt about something (you do not know what is in that bag), say "저 가방 안에 뭐가 있을까요?" ("I wonder what is in that bag") rather than "뭐가 있어요?" ("What is in the bag?") because you are not directly asking someone. You are simply just showing your curiosity.

Even when suggesting to do something together with someone, use the -(으)ㄹ까요? ending if you are not sure. For example, you are not sure if you want to see a movie with your friend, so you ask him/her "영화 볼까요?" In this way, you are expressing your curiosity about what your friend wants to do and your own uncertainty, and at the same time, suggesting or inviting your friend to the movies in case he/she wants to go.

This is the most fundamental usage of -(으)ㄹ까요? There are three basic levels of usage: to ask someone a question, to ask yourself a question, and to make a declarative sentence expressing wonder, curiosity, or uncertainty.

Sample Sentences

내일 비가 올까요?

= Do you think it will rain tomorrow?

= I wonder if it will rain tomorrow.

= Will it rain tomorrow? What do you think?

(It CANNOT mean "shall we..." because "Shall we ... rain tomorrow?" does not make sense.)

Track 07

내일 우리 영화 볼까요?

= Shall we see a movie tomorrow?

= Do you want to see a movie together tomorrow?

(It CANNOT mean "I wonder if..." because "Do you assume that we will see a movie tomorrow?" generally does not make sense.)

이 사람은 누구일까요?

= Who do you think this person is?

= Who is this person, I wonder?

= I wonder who this person is.

우유 마실까요? 주스 마실까요?

= Shall we drink milk? Shall we drink juice?

= Do you want to drink milk or juice?

Construction for the past tense

Add the past tense suffix -았/었/였- right after the verb stem and before -(으)ㄹ까요 to make an assumption about a past event. Since this is in the past tense, it can ONLY be used for expressing doubt or curiosity.

Sample Sentences

어제 했을까요?

= Do you think she did it yesterday?

Track 07

누가 전화했을까요?

= Who do you think called?

어제 탈리아나가 한국에 왔을까요?

= Do you think Taliana came to Korea yesterday?

Sample Dialogue

Track
08

A: 지금 바빠요? 이따가 올까요?

B: 아니요. 지금 시간 있어요.
   여기 앉으세요.

A: 네.

A: *Are you busy now? Shall I come
   later?*

B: *No. I have time now. Please take
   a seat here.*

A: *Okay.*

✏ Exercises for Lesson 4

1. If 보다 means "to see", how do you say "Shall we see?" in Korean?

(   )

2. If 팔다 means "to sell", how do you write "Shall we sell?" in Korean?

(   )

3. How do you say "Do you think it will rain tomorrow?/ I wonder if it will rain tomorrow./ Will it rain tomorrow? What do you think?"

내일 비가 (   ) ?

4. How do you say "Do you want to drink milk or juice?/ Shall we drink milk? Shall we drink juice?"
   * 마시다 = to drink

(   )

5. In Korean, please write "Shall we see a movie tomorrow?"

(   )

Check the answers on **p.196**

LESSON 5

Approximately, About

-쯤, 정도, 약

In this lesson, you will learn how to say "approximately" or "about" when talking quantity, frequency, time, and so on. There are many different ways to say this in Korean, but the most commonly used expression is **-쯤**.

In English, "about", "approximately", and "around" are used BEFORE nouns. However, in Korean, the word -쯤 is used AFTER nouns.

Ex)
1 o'clock = 한 시
Around 1 o'clock = 한 시쯤

1,000 won = 천 원
About 1,000 won = 천 원쯤

One month = 한 달

34

Approximately one month = 한 달쯤

4 kilometers = 4킬로미터
About 4 kilometers = 4킬로미터쯤

Similar expressions : 정도, 약

-쯤, 정도 are used after nouns, whereas 약 is used BEFORE nouns.

한 달 = one month
한 달쯤 = about a month
한 달 정도 = about a month
약 한 달 = about a month

Track 09

* Note that 정도 has a space before it and 쯤 does not. Sometimes people also use 약 and 쯤 together or 약 and 정도 together.

약 한 달쯤 = about a month
약 한 달 정도 = about a month

Sample Sentences
100명쯤 왔어요.
= About 100 people came.

by Learning Irregularities, Linking Verbs, Politeness Levels, and Much More

독일에서 2년쯤 살았어요.

= I lived in Germany for about two years.

언제쯤 갈 거예요?

= Approximately when are you going to go?

내일 몇 시쯤 만날까요?

= Around what time shall we meet tomorrow?

다섯 시쯤 어때요?

= How about around five o'clock?

Track 09

Sample Dialogue

Track 10

A: 현우 씨는 언제 와요?

B: 밥 먹고 두 시쯤에 올 거예요.

A: 저희는 지금 밥 먹을까요?

A: When does Hyunwoo come?

B: He is going to come around 2 o'clock after he eats.

A: Shall we eat now then?

by Learning Irregularities, Linking Verbs, Politeness Levels, and Much More

✐ Exercises for Lesson 5

Check the answers on **p.196**

1. What is the word for "approximately" or "about" when talking about quantity, frequency, time, and so on, in Korean?

(   )

2. How do you write "about a month" in Korean if "one month" is 한 달?

(   )

3. How do you say "About when are you going to go?" in Korean?

(   )

4. If "to meet" is 만나다 and "tomorrow" is 내일 in Korean, how do you write "Around what time shall we meet tomorrow?"

(   )

5. "To live" is 살다 in Korean. How do you write "I lived in Korea for about two years"?

(   )

LESSON **6**

Future Tense

-(으)ㄹ 거예요 VS. -(으)ㄹ게요

🎙 Track 11

In Level 2, Lesson 1, you learned how to use the verb ending -(으)ㄹ 거예요 to express future tense. In this lesson, you will learn one more way to express future tense and how it differs from -(으)ㄹ 거예요.

-(으)ㄹ 거예요 vs. -(으)ㄹ게요

If pronouncing -(으)ㄹ 거예요 very quickly, it sounds similar to -(으)ㄹ게요. Many beginner-level, and even advanced-level learners mix up these two endings often, but these two sentence endings for the future are actually used for two distinctively different purposes.

Take a look at -(으)ㄹ 거예요 first.

-(으)ㄹ 거예요 is the most basic way to express a future plan or action. To use this ending, attach it to the end of a verb stem.

39

하다 = to do

하 + -ㄹ 거예요 = 할 거예요 = I will do _____. / I am going to do _____.

보내다 = to send

보내 + -ㄹ 거예요 = 보낼 거예요 = I will send _____. / I am going to send _____.

웃다 = to laugh

웃 + -을 거예요 = 웃을 거예요 = I will laugh.

-(으)ㄹ 거예요 is used to express intention or plan for a future action or expectation for a future state. This is NOT related to or affected by the reaction or the request of the other person in the conversation.

Track 11

For example, if someone asked about your plans for the weekend, you would say "친구들 만날 거예요" ("I am going to meet my friends") because you are planning to meet your friends no matter what the person who asked you says.

Now, take a look at -(으)ㄹ게요.

-(으)ㄹ게요 is also attached to the end of a verb stem and also expresses the future, but it focuses more on actions or decisions AS A REACTION TO or AS A RESULT OF what the other person says or thinks.

Compare -(으)ㄹ 거예요 and -(으)ㄹ게요

I. 할 거예요 vs. **할게요**

공부할 거예요.

= I am going to study.

= I will study.

* Regardless of what the other person says, you were ALREADY planning to study, and the other person will not change your mind.

> **Ex)**
> 방해하지 마세요. 공부할 거예요.
> = Do not disturb me. I will study.

Track 11

공부할게요.

= I will study.

= (If you say so,) I will study.

= (Since the circumstances are like this,) I will study.

= (If you do not mind,) I will study.

* This is a response to something another person has said to you. Whatever the other person said has made you think, "Oh, in that case, I have to study." However, you could also say this before the other person says anything, but you usually need to wait for the other person's reaction to see if he/she has anything to say.

Ex)

알았어요. 공부할게요.

= (After assessing the atmosphere) Okay. I will study.

2. 갈 거예요 vs. 갈게요

저도 갈 거예요.

= I will go (there), too.

= I am going to go, too.

= I am coming along, as well.

저도 갈게요.

Track 11

= I will come along, too (if you do not mind).

= (In that case,) I will go there, too.

= (Okay, since you say so,) I will go, too.

To summarize, use -(으)ㄹ게요 when:

1. changing plans according to what the other person said;

2. checking or assuming what the other person thinks by saying something using this ending and seeing his/her reaction;

3. deciding to do something because of what the other person said.

Sample Sentences

지금 어디예요? 지금 나갈게요.

= Where are you now? I will go out now. (+ if you do not mind / if you want me to / unless you do not want me to / what do you think about that?)

* You cannot use "지금 나갈 거예요" here because it means that you were already going out anyway, and more than likely to an unrelated place, regardless of where the other person is located.

저 갈게요. 안녕히 계세요.

= I am going to go. Take care. (+ unless you want me to stay longer / unless there is something I have to stay longer to do)

    * You cannot use "저 갈 거예요" because it is implying that you do not care whether or not the other person wants you to stay because you are leaving anyway. You would only say it when you do not want the other person to ask you to stay because you have absolutely no intention of staying even if you are asked.

그래요? 다시 할게요.

= Is that so? I will do it again.

Track 11

    * If you say "다시 할 거예요" here instead of "다시 할게요" implies that you were already aware of the problem and you were going to do it again anyway. This comes off as a little insulting.

내일 4시쯤에 갈게요. 괜찮아요?

= I will be there at around 4 o'clock tomorrow. Is that alright?

    * By saying "내일 4시쯤에 갈 거예요" here instead, you are implying that you do not care what the other person thinks nor do you care if going at 4 o'clock will affect the other person's schedule; therefore, you do not care if it is okay or not, which makes you sound rude.

Sample Dialogue

Track
12

A: 방 청소했어요?

B: 아니요, 아직 안 했어요.

A: 언제 할 거예요?

B: 지금 할게요.

A: Have you cleaned your room?

B: No, I haven't done yet.

A: When are you going to do it?

B: I will do it now.

✏ *Exercises for Lesson 6*

1. Which of the following would you use if you want to convey the meaning of "I'm going to study / I'll study regardless of what others are thinking or planning to do"?

    a. 공부할 거예요.   b. 공부할게요.

2. Choose the phrase which best translates to the following: "I will also come along (if you don't mind) / (In that case,) I will go there, too / (Okay, since you say so,) I will go, too."

    a. 저도 갈 거예요.   b. 저도 갈게요.

3. If someone asked you about your plans for the weekend, how do you say "I'm going to meet my friends" in Korean?

    a. 친구들 만날게요.   b. 친구들 만날 거예요.

4. Write "Where are you now? I will go out now (if you don't mind / if you want me to / unless you don't want me to)."

    * 지금 = now

    (   )

5. Translate the following sentence into Korean: "Is that so? I'll do it again."

    * 다시 = again

    (   )

Check the answers on **p.196**

45

LESSON 7

Linking Verbs

-아/어/여서

Track 13

Back in Lesson 2 of this level, you learned about the verb ending -고, which is used to connect independent clauses or actions together to form one sentence; even though the two clauses may not necessarily have a strong logical relation to each other. In this lesson, you will learn the verb ending -아/어/여+서 which connects two or more verbs in one sentence and can show a logical relationship between the verbs.

Do you remember the two conjunctions 그리고 and 그래서 from Level 2, Lesson 3?

그리고 means "and", and 그래서 means "therefore" or "so".

The verb ending -고 has the same meaning as 그리고, and the verb ending -아/어/여+서 is similar in meaning to 그래서.

Take a look at the construction and usages of **-아/어/여+서** in more detail:

> *Conjugation*
>
> 1. verb stems ending in vowels ㅏ or ㅗ + -아서
> 2. verb stems ending in other vowels + -어서
> 3. 하 + -여서

Ex)

먹다 = to eat

먹 (verb stem) + -어서 = 먹어서

만들다 = to make

만들 (verb stem) + -어서 = 만들어서

Track 13

하다 = to do

하 (verb stem) + -여서 = 해서

오다 = to come

오 (verb stem) + -아서 = 와서

Usages

1. Reason + -아/어/여서 + result
2. An action + -아/어/여서 + another action which takes place after the first action
3. An action + -아/어/여서 + the purpose of or the plan after the action
4. Fixed expressions

47

Usage #1

Reason + -아/어/여서 + result

Ex)

비가 오다 (it rains) + 못 가다 (cannot go)

→ 비가 와서 못 가요. = It is raining, so I cannot go.

→ 비가 와서 못 갔어요. = It rained, so I could not go.

* Note that the tense was expressed only through the final verb.

오늘은 바빠요. (Today, I am busy.) + 영화를 못 봐요. (I cannot see the movie.)

→ 오늘은 바빠서 영화를 못 봐요.

= I am busy today, so I cannot see the movie.

Track 13

만나다 (to meet) + 반갑다 (to be glad to see someone)

→ 만나서 반갑습니다.

= I met you, so I am glad. = It is nice to meet you.

→ 만나서 반가워요.

= I am pleased to meet you. (Less formal than the sentence above)

Usage #2

An action + -아/어/여서 + another action that takes place after the first action

Ex)

공원에 가다 (to go to the park) + 책을 읽다 (to read a book)

→ 공원에 가서 책을 읽을 거예요.

= I am going to go to the park and read a book.

* *Note:* This does NOT mean "I am going to the park, so I am going to read a book."

** Also note that the tense is only used with the final verb here as well.

친구를 만나다 (to meet a friend) + 밥을 먹다 (to eat)

→ 친구를 만나서 밥을 먹었어요.

= I met a friend, and (we) ate together.

* This sentence COULD mean that you met a friend, so you ate together. In most cases, however, it means that you met a friend THEN ate together after you met up with him/her.

→ 친구를 만나서 밥을 먹을 거예요.

= I am going to meet a friend, and (we will) eat together.

Usage #3
An action + -아/어/여서 + the purpose of or the plan after the action

Track
13

Ex)

돈을 모으다 (to save up, to save money) + 뭐 하다 (to do what)

→ 돈을 모아서 뭐 할 거예요?

= What are you going to do with the money you save up? (lit. You save up money and what will you do?)

케이크를 사다 (to buy a cake) + 친구한테 주다 (to give to a friend)

→ 케이크를 사서 친구한테 줄 거예요.

= I am going to buy a cake to/and give it to a friend.

* Usage 3 is similar to Usage 2 because the events are happening one after the other, so it could be a linear action, and it could also be a purpose.

49

Usage #4

Fixed expressions

There are a couple of fixed expressions which basically use the same -아/어/여서 structure but are not often used in other forms.

-에 따라서 = according to ~

Ex)

계획에 따라서 진행하겠습니다

= I will proceed according to the plan.

Track 13

예를 들어서 = for example

Ex)

예를 들어서, 이렇게 할 수 있어요.

= For example, you can do it like this.

Sample Sentences

한국에 가서 뭐 할 거예요?

= After you go to Korea, what are you going to do?

서울에 와서 좋아요.

= Since I came to Seoul, I am glad.

= I am glad to have come to Seoul.

잠을 많이 자서 전혀 피곤하지 않아요.

= I slept a lot, so I am not tired at all.

비가 와서 집에 있었어요.

= It rained, so I stayed at home.

요즘에 바빠서 친구들을 못 만나요.

= These days I am busy, so I cannot meet my friends.

열심히 공부해서 장학금을 받을 거예요.

= I am going to study hard so I can get (and I will get) a scholarship.

한국어가 너무 재미있어서 매일 공부하고 있어요.

= Korean is so much fun that I am studying it every day.

Track 13

by Learning Irregularities, Linking Verbs, Politeness Levels, and Much More

Sample Dialogue

Track 14

A: 한국어보다 중국어가 더 쉬워요?

B: 네, 중국어가 더 쉬워요.

A: 왜요?

B: 영어랑 비슷해서요.

A: Is Chinese easier than Korean?

B: Yes. Chinese is easier.

A: Why?

B: That is because it is similar to English.

✎ Exercises for Lesson 7

Review: -아/어/여+서 *is a verb ending that can show logical relation between verbs.* 그리고 *means* "and", *and* 그래서 *means* "therefore/so". *The verb ending* -고 *has the same meaning as* 그리고, *and the verb ending* -아/어/여+서 *has a similar meaning as* 그래서.

Please answer the following questions in Korean:

1. 하다 = to do

하 (verb stem) + 여서 = (   )

2. 먹다 = to eat

먹 (verb stem) + 어서 = (   )

3. 오다 = to come

오 (verb stem) + 아서 = (   )

Match the English with its Korean equivalent.

4. according to ~   a. 예를 들어서

5. for example   b. 재미있어서

                             c. -에 따라서

Check the answers on **p.196**

by Learning Irregularities, Linking Verbs, Politeness Levels, and Much More

LESSON **8**

To look like, To seem like (used with nouns)

같다

Track
15

By the end of this lesson, you will be able to say and write sentences such as "You are like an angel", "This looks like coffee", or "You are similar to my teacher."

First, take a look at how to express that something is similar to something else.

비슷하다 = to be similar

- Present tense: 비슷해요 = it is similar

To say "A is similar to B" in Korean, the particle which means "with" or "together with" is needed. Do you remember which particle that is? It's -(이)랑 or -하고. (Go back to Level 2 Lesson 4 to review if you have forgotten!)

A랑 비슷해요. = It is similar to A.
B하고 비슷해요. = It is similar to B.

Ex)

도쿄는 서울하고 비슷해요?

= Is Tokyo similar to Seoul?

참외는 멜론하고 비슷해요.

= Chamoe (Korean melon) is similar to melon.

Now look at the word for "to be the same" in Korean.

같다 = to be the same

- Present tense: 같아요 = it is the same, they are the same

Track 15

In English, when saying "A is the same as B", the word "as" is needed. In Korean, -(이)랑 or -하고 is used here as well.

A랑 같아요. = It is the same as A.

A하고 B는 같아요. = A and B are the same.

Ex)

이거랑 이거랑 같아요?

= Is this the same as this? / Are these two things the same?

So, -(이)랑/하고 비슷하다 and -(이)랑/하고 같다 are used to express that something is similar to, or the same as something else, in Korean!

55

There is another frequent usage of 같다, which means "to be like Noun." In this usage, the noun followed by 같다 is mostly used by itself without any particles attached.

> **Conjugation**
>
> Noun + 같다 = to be like + Noun / to look like + Noun / to seem to be + Noun

Ex)

커피 같아요.

= It is like coffee. / It seems to be coffee. / It looks like coffee.

거짓말 같아요.

= It seems to be a lie. / It sounds like a lie.

로봇 같아요.

= It is like a robot. / It seems to be a robot. / It looks like a robot.

Track 15

Sample Sentences

저 사람은 로봇 같아요.

= That person is like a robot.

경은 씨는 천사 같아요.

= Kyeong-eun is like an angel.

현우 씨는 천재 같아요.

= Hyunwoo seems to be a genius.

그 이야기는 거짓말 같아요.

= That story sounds like a lie.

이 강아지는 고양이 같아요.

= This puppy is like a cat.

Although this lesson only covered how to use 같아요 with nouns, in the next lesson, you will build upon that knowledge and learn to use 같아요 with verbs so you can say more things in Korean!

Track 15

Sample Dialogue

A: 이 원숭이는 너무 똑똑해서
　　사람 같아요.

B: 맞아요.

A: 그래서 좀 무섭기도 해요.

A: *This monkey is so smart that it looks
　　like a person.*

B: *That's right.*

A: *It also makes me a little scared.*

✏ Exercises for Lesson 8

1. What is "to be similar" in Korean?

( )

2. Write "We are the same age" in Korean.
   * 같다 = to be the same

( )

3. Translate the following sentence to Korean: "Is this the same as this?"

( )

4. Write "It's like coffee / It seems to be coffee / It looks like coffee" in Korean.

( )

5. Write "That story sounds like a lie" in Korean.
   * 거짓말 = a lie

( )

Check the answers on **p.196**

by Learning Irregularities, Linking Verbs, Politeness Levels, and Much More

LESSON 9

To look like, To seem like (used with verbs)

-(으)ㄴ/는/(으)ㄹ 것 같아요

Track 17

In the previous lesson, you learned how to use 같아요 with nouns to mean "it looks like" or "it seems to be".

Ex)

커피 같아요.

= It looks like coffee. / I think it is coffee.

저 사람 소연 씨 같아요.

= That person looks like So-yeon. / I think that person is So-yeon.

In the examples above, both 커피 and 소연 씨 are nouns. The usage of 같아요 is fairly simple and straightforward: just add 같아요 after the noun.

When using 같아요 with verbs, however, the verb needs to be changed into its noun form. There are a few different ways to change a verb into a noun, but here, -는 것 form will be used. (If you studied with the Level 2 book, you learned how to use -는 것 in Lesson 19!)

60

1. Descriptive verbs

Verb stem + -(으)ㄴ 것

Ex)

예쁘다 = to be pretty

예쁜 것 = being pretty; something pretty; the thing that is pretty

2. Action verbs

Present tense
Verb stem + -는 것

Track 17

Ex)

말하다 = to talk, to speak; to say

말하는 것 = talking; what one is saying; the act of talking

Past tense
Verb stem + -(으)ㄴ 것

Ex)

말한 것 = what one said; the fact that one talked

Future tense
Verb stem + -(으)ㄹ 것

Ex)

말할 것 = what one will say; the fact that one will talk

How to use 같아요 with verbs

Okay! Now that you know how to change verbs into the –(으)ㄴ/는 것 noun form, you are
ready to take the next step. After changing a verb into its noun form, add 같아요 after 것. It
is exactly the same as using 같아요 with nouns.

-(으)ㄴ 것 같아요

= present tense for descriptive verbs / past tense for action verbs

-는 것 같아요

= present tense for action verbs

-(으)ㄹ 것 같아요

= future tense for action / descriptive verbs

What does - 것 같아요 mean?

Even when 같아요 is combined with a verb, since - 것 makes the verb a noun, the basic
meaning and usage is the same as "Noun + 같아요".

1. "It looks like..."
2. "It seems to be..."

3. "To me it looks like..."

4. "I think it is..."

5. "I think it will..."

6. "I think it was..."

Ex)

이상하다 = to be strange

이상하 + ㄴ 것 같아요 = 이상한 것 같아요.

= It seems to be strange. / I think it is strange.

눈이 오다 = to snow

눈이 오 + 는 것 같아요 = 눈이 오는 것 같아요.

= It seems to be snowing. / I think it is snowing.

Track 17

눈이 오 + ㄹ 것 같아요 = 눈이 올 것 같아요.

= I think it will snow. / It seems like it will snow.

이야기하다 = to tell; to talk

이야기하 + ㄴ 것 같아요 = 이야기한 것 같아요.

= I think they told them. / It looks like they talked.

이야기하 + ㄹ 것 같아요 = 이야기할 것 같아요.

= I think they will talk. / It seems like they will talk.

이야기하 + 는 것 같아요 = 이야기하는 것 같아요.

= I think they are talking. / They seem to talk to each other.

As seen in the examples above, - 것 같아요 can also be used to mean "I think" in Korean. In fact, this phrase is used so often in Korean that it is almost guaranteed you will come across it when interacting with native speakers.

63

Sample Sentences

여기 비싼 것 같아요.

= I think this place is expensive.

= This place looks expensive.

= This place seems to be expensive.

그런 것 같아요.

= I think so.

= It seems to be so.

= It looks like it.

* Verb = 그렇다 (irregular) = to be so; to be that way

Track 17

이 영화 재미있을 것 같아요.

= I think this movie will be interesting.

= This movie looks like it will be interesting (to watch).

이 가방, 여기에서 산 것 같아요.

= This bag seems like we bought it here.

= I think I bought this bag here.

아마 안 할 것 같아요.

= I think I probably will not do it.

= It looks like we are probably not going to do it.

Sample Dialogue

Track 18

A: 여기 맛있을 것 같아요.

B: 맞아요.

A: 근데 좀 비쌀 것 같아요.

A: *I think the food here will be good.*

B: *I think so, too.*

A: *But, I think it will be a little pricey.*

by Learning Irregularities, Linking Verbs, Politeness Levels, and Much More

✏ *Exercises for Lesson* **9**

* *"To tell"* or *"to talk"* is **이야기하다** *in Korean.*

Match the English sentence to its Korean equivalent.

1. I think they told them. /
It looks like they talked.

a. 이야기할 것 같아요.

2. I think they are talking. /
They seem to talk to each other.

b. 이야기한 것 같아요.

3. I think they will talk. /
It seems like they will talk.

c. 이야기하는 것 같아요.

4. Write "I think this place is expensive / It looks expensive / This place seems to be expensive"
in Korean.
* To be expensive = 비싸다

(   )

5. Translate the following to Korean: "I think so / It seems to be so / It looks like it."
* To be so; to be that way = 그렇다

(   )

Check the answers on **p.197**

66

LESSON **10**

Before -ing

-기 전에

In this lesson, you will learn how to say and use -기 전에 in sentences to express "before -ing" in Korean. As with many Korean expressions and prepositions, the order is the opposite of English. In English, the word "before" comes before the clause or word, but in Korean, it comes after.

Track 19

The key syllable here is 전. The Chinese character for 전 is 前, and it means "before", "front", or "earlier". To this, add the particle -에 to make it a preposition (a word which shows the relationship between the noun or pronoun and other words in the sentence).

전에 = before (+ noun)

수업 전에 = before class
일요일 전에 = before Sunday
1시 전에 = before 1 o'clock

Since 전에 is used after nouns, in order to use it with verbs such as "going" or "leaving", the verbs need to be changed into nouns.

In the previous lesson, to use verbs before 같다, the verbs were changed into their noun forms by using -(으)ㄴ/는 것. In this case, however, -기 is used to change the verbs into nouns. (Do you remember this? If not, take a minute to go back and review Level 2, Lesson 14!)

가다 → 가기 (going)   → 가기 전에 = before going

사다 → 사기 (buying)   + 전에 → 사기 전에 = before buying

먹다 → 먹기 (eating)   → 먹기 전에 = before eating

Ex)

집에 가다 = to go home

→ 집에 가기 전에

   = before going home; before you go home

공부하다 = to study

→ 공부하기 전에

   = before studying; before you study

돈을 내다 = to pay money

→ 돈을 내기 전에

   = before paying money; before you pay money

68

Sample Sentences

여기 오기 전에 뭐 했어요?

= What were you doing before you came here?

친구들하고 놀기 전에 숙제할 거예요.

= I am going to do homework before I hang out with (my) friends.

  * 친구들하고 놀다 = to hang out with one's friends

들어오기 전에 노크하세요.

= Knock before you come in.

  * 들어오다 = to come in

사기 전에 잘 생각하세요.

= Think well before you buy it.

  * 사다 = to buy

Track 19

도망가기 전에 잡으세요.

= Catch him before he runs away.

  * 도망가다 = to run away

by Learning Irregularities, Linking Verbs, Politeness Levels, and Much More

Sample Dialogue

Track 20

A: 밥 먹고 운동할 거예요.

B: 밥 먹기 전에 운동하는 것이 더 좋아요.

A: 정말요? 몰랐어요.

A: I will work out after I eat.

B: It is better to work out before you have a meal.

A: Really? I didn't know that.

✎ Exercises for Lesson 10

1. How do you write "before (+noun)" in Korean?

( )

2. Write "before studying / before you study" in Korean.

( )

3. Write "before paying money / before you pay money" in Korean.

   * To pay money = 돈을 내다

( )

4. Translate the following sentence to Korean: "Knock before you come in."

   * 들어오다 = to come in

( )

5. Write "Think well before you buy" in Korean.

   * To buy = 사다

( )

Check the answers on **p.197**

by Learning Irregularities, Linking Verbs, Politeness Levels, and Much More

BLOG

DAEHAKRO
(대학로)

대학로 (Dae-hak-ro) means "college street". It's actually pronounced 대항노 (dae-hang-no), which is slightly different than the "official" romanization. This is because of a tricky little Hangeul pronunciation rule:

When the letter ㄱ is the 받침 (final consonant) of a syllable and is followed by ㄹ, the pronunciation of ㄱ changes to ㅇ, and the pronunciation of ㄹ becomes ㄴ.
This is mostly for ease of pronunciation because it's WAY easier to say 대항노 than it is to try and spit out 대학로 at native speed. Plus, no one will know what you're talking about if you pronounce it as "dae-hak-ro."

Some other examples of this rule are:
독립 (independence) → 동닙
석류 (pomegranate) → 성뉴
목련 (magnolia) → 몽년

73

It may seem a little confusing at first, but once you start practicing, you'll find that it just naturally comes out this way.

Anyway, now that we have that out of the way, let's learn more about 대학로!

대학로 used to be the main road that bordered Seoul National University's College of Arts and Sciences. Although that campus moved to another part of the city some time ago, 대학로 is still the core of about a half dozen major university branches. It is also known as the "street of youth, art, and freedom", and from this name, it may seem that only younger people frequent the streets of 대학로. That is certainly not the case. 대학로 is more of an intersection where the youth of today and the youth of half a generation ago meet to explore and share what is quintessentially Korea: tradition and modernity.

One of the best spots to experience this generational crossroad is 마로니에 공원 (Marronnier Park). 마로니에 공원 used to be the campus of Seoul National University's College of Arts and Sciences but has since become a terrific cultural space. At the center of 마로니에 공원 is a symbolic 밤나무 (marronnier/chestnut tree), and surrounding it are dozens of sculptures and art centers. This place is particularly good for hanging out on the weekends because of the numerous bands, singers, comedians, and dance troupes that gather here to give performances. You may also run into a few street artists who will draw your picture for a small price, or even a fortuneteller who may unveil your future :D

This area is famous for being a "theater district" since there is a high concentration of theaters and concert halls. If you like comedy, you can find live comedy shows here as well, the most famous being the live version of KBS's famous comedy show

"Gag Concert". How's that for famous? At any rate, you can find posters for various productions hanging up all over the streets of 대학로. This neighborhood is definitely one of the best places in Seoul to experience plays and musicals that are sometimes neither huge productions nor are they very expensive.

Although 대학로 is more of a theater district, there are a good number of international restaurants, cafes, cinemas, jazz bars, and some small stores at which to shop. Since it's a college area, everything is really cheap compared to some other places in the city. Whether you're looking to try some 파전 (Korean pancake) with your friends or want to purchase some skin care products, you will definitely get your money's worth at 대학로!

With former Prime Minister Chang Myeon's house, the Hyehwa-dong Residence Center, the first President of Korea's former residence, and a number of other cultural experiences, 대학로 also has a lot of history behind it. It's also just a stone's throw away from 낙산 (Naksan), the Seoul Fortress Wall, and 동대문 (The Great East Gate) which makes it a SUPER good place to start exploring Seoul.

This blog post just scratched the surface of all that 대학로 has to offer, so make sure to get your happy little self over here to experience it first-hand.

Thanks for reading the blog,
and good luck with the rest of Level 3!

LESSON **11**

Irregulars: ㅂ

ㅂ 불규칙

Track 21

If you have been studying with this book series from Level 1, you have learned so much about the different conjugations, rules, and usages for Korean verbs. In fact, you may have expanded your vocabulary with a number of verbs too! Yay! Congratulations! However, there is always more to learn, so keep up the good work! Just as in many other languages, Korean has some irregularities which, over the course of time, were used more and more, and eventually, became a fixed rule.

Korean has much fewer verb irregularities than some other languages, but you will encounter these irregularities everywhere as you learn more and start speaking more Korean. One irregularity in Korean is conjugating verb stems which end in ㅂ.

Irregular ㅂ

This means that if a verb has ㅂ at the end of the verb stem, and it is followed by a suffix which starts with a vowel, the ㅂ will change to 오 or 우.

77

Conjugation

If the vowel before ㅂ is 오, change ㅂ to 오.

If the vowel before ㅂ is not 오, change ㅂ to 우.

Ex)

돕다 = to help

= 도 + ㅂ + 다 → 도 + 오 + 아요 = 도와요

* Note that it is NOT 돕아요.

[present tense] 도와요

[past tense] 도왔어요

[future tense] 도울 거예요

어렵다 = to be difficult

= 어려 + ㅂ + 다 → 어려 + 우 + 어요 = 어려워요

[present tense] 어려워요

[past tense] 어려웠어요

[future tense] 어려울 거예요

춥다 = to be cold → 추 + 우 + 어요 = 추워요

[present tense] 추워요

[past tense] 추웠어요

[future tense] 추울 거예요

Some other irregular words

눕다 = to lie down → 누워요.

굽다 = to bake → 구워요.

덥다 = to be hot (weather) → 더워요.

쉽다 = to be easy → 쉬워요.

맵다 = to be spicy → 매워요.

귀엽다 = to be cute → 귀여워요.

밉다 = to hate; to be dislikeable → 미워요.

아름답다 = to be beautiful → 아름다워요.

Remember that these verbs have irregular forms ONLY WHEN the suffix following the verb stem starts with a VOWEL. Therefore, with suffixes such as -는 or -고, ㅂ does not change.

Track 21

Ex)

돕다 = to help → 돕 + -는 것 = 돕는 것

Irregularities in irregular verbs

Although the ㅂ irregular rule is applied to most verbs which contain ㅂ as a 받침 (final consonant) in the verb stem, there are a handful of verbs which do not follow this rule.

Action verbs:

- 입다 = to wear

- 잡다 = to catch

- 씹다 = to bite

79

Descriptive verbs:

- 좁다 = to be narrow

- 넓다 = to be wide

The ㅂ in these words does not change when in front of a vowel.

Ex)

입다 → 입어요 (Not 이워요)

좁다 → 좁아요 (Not 조아요)

Sample Sentences

Track 21

이 문제는 어려워요.

= This problem is difficult.

이거 너무 귀여워요.

= This is so cute.

서울은 겨울에 정말 추워요.

= In Seoul, it is really cold in the winter.

TTMIK으로 공부하면, 한국어 공부가 쉬워요.

= If you study with TTMIK, studying Korean is easy.

Sample Dialogue

A: 석진 씨, 추워요? 에어컨 끌까요?

B: 네, 꺼 주세요.

A: 껐어요. 너무 더우면 말하세요.

A: *Seokjin, are you cold? Do you want me to turn off the air conditioner?*

B: *Yes, please.*

A: *I've turned it off. Please let me know if it gets too hot.*

by Learning Irregularities, Linking Verbs, Politeness Levels, and Much More

✏ Exercises for Lesson 11

Check the answers on **p.197**

1. Since the ㅂ in the verb 돕다 (to help) is irregular, it changes to 도와요. Not all verbs have an irregular ㅂ. Please choose the verb from the list below which does not have an irregular ㅂ.

    a. 입다 = to wear

    b. 눕다 = to lie down

    c. 춥다 = to be cold

    d. 쉽다 = to be easy

2. "To be difficult" is 어렵다 in Korean. Present tense for 어렵다 is 어려워요. What is the past tense form?

    a. 어려울 거예요   b. 어려웠어요

Write following sentences in Korean:

3. This is so cute!   * 귀엽다 = to be cute

    (   )

4. This problem is difficult.   * 어렵다 = to be difficult

    (   )

5. In Seoul, it's really cold in the winter.   * 춥다 = to be cold

    (   )

LESSON 12

But still, Nevertheless

> # 그래도

Are you ready to learn more Korean conjunctions? Yes! Good answer!

Track 23

You will learn how to connect two sentences with the word **그래도** in this lesson, so put your thinking cap on and let's get started!

In Level 2, Lesson 3, you learned how to use 그래서, which means "so" or "therefore". The only difference in spelling of 그래서 and 그래도 is the final syllable, but that one little 도 gives the word an entirely different meaning.

그래도 means "but still", "however", "nonetheless", or "nevertheless".

Ex)
비가 와요. 그래도 갈 거예요?

= It is raining. Are you still going?

83

Let's break it down:

그래도 = 그래 + 도

그래 = 그렇게 해 or 그렇게 하여 (to do it in such a way, to do that)

-도 = also, too, even

The literal meaning of "그래 + 도" is "even if you do that", "even if that happens", or "if you do that, too" with the meaning of "still" added to the context.

Sample Sentences

한국어는 어려워요. 그래도 재미있어요.

= Korean is difficult. But still, it is interesting.

Track 23

어제는 비가 왔어요. 그래도 축구를 했어요.

= Yesterday, it rained. Nevertheless, we played soccer.

저도 돈이 없어요. 그래도 걱정하지 마세요.

= I do not have money, either. But still, do not worry.

노래방에 가야 돼요. 그래도 노래 안 할 거예요.

= I have to go to a noraebang (singing room). However, I am not going to sing.

요즘 바빠요. 그래도 한국어를 공부하고 있어요.

= I am busy these days. But I am still studying Korean.

그래도 can also be used as an interjection when speaking with friends and you just want to say, "But still..." or "Come on...".

If you feel the need to be more polite, or if you want to make 100% sure you are not being rude, add -요 to the end and say, "그래도요". The "도요" combination takes a bit of work to pronounce, so you may find that other people, especially women in Seoul, end up saying "그래두요" rather than "그래도요" (like the change in pronunciation of -고 to "구" as mentioned in Lesson 2 of this book).

Track 23

Sample Dialogue

Track 24

A: 주연 씨, 화장 안 했어요?

B: 네. 늦게 일어나서 화장 안 하고
  왔어요.

A: 그래도 너무 예뻐요.

A: *You have no makeup on, Jooyeon?*

B: *No. Since I got up late, I didn't put on
  any makeup.*

A: *But you are still so pretty.*

✏ Exercises for Lesson 12

1. How do you say "but still", "however", or "nonetheless" in Korean?

(   )

Fill in the blanks with the appropriate Korean word to complete the sentence.

2. 노래방에 가야 돼요. (   ) 노래 안 할 거예요.

= I have to go to a noraebang (singing room). But still, I'm not going to sing.

3. 어제는 (   ). (   ) 축구를 했어요.

= Yesterday, it rained. But still, we played soccer.
  * To play soccer = 축구를 하다

4. 한국어는 (   ). (   ) 재미있어요.

= Korean is difficult. But still, it's interesting.
  * To be interesting = 재미있다

Check the answers on **p.197**

LESSON 13

Making Adjectives (Part 1)

adjectives in infinitive form **+ -(으)ㄴ + 명사**

Korean and English are different in many ways - one key difference being "adjectives". For example, in English, "beautiful" is an adjective and can be looked up in the dictionary just as it is. Translated directly to Korean as an adjective, "beautiful" is 예쁜, which cannot be found in the dictionary. The "descriptive verb" form, or the "adjective in infinitive form", of 예쁜, which is 예쁘다 (to be beautiful), however, can be found in the dictionary.

"To be + adjective" is known as "infinitive form" in English, but when studying Korean, often at times it is referred to as "descriptive verb form". Both terms essentially mean the same thing, so do not worry too much about the terminology!

Ex)

싸다 → It does NOT mean "cheap". It means "to be cheap".

바쁘다 → It does NOT mean "busy". It means "to be busy".

맛있다 → It does NOT mean "delicious". It means "to be delicious".

By the end of this lesson, you will be well acquainted with recognizing the difference between an "adjective" and an "adjective in infinitive form" in Korean, as well as being able to use each form correctly.

"Adjectives in infinitive form" have the ability to be conjugated just as any "action verb" (the main reason why they are commonly referred to as "descriptive verbs"). The actual "adjective", on the other hand, never changes form.

For example, the word "fun" in English is always "fun" no matter what the tense is: "It is fun" (present tense), "It was fun" (past tense), or "It will be fun" (future tense). In Korean, since "adjectives in the infinitive form" can be conjugated, 재미있다 (to be fun) is conjugated to 재미있어요 (present tense), 재미있었어요 (past tense), and 재미있을 거예요 (future tense).

Track 25

What if I want to use "adjectives in the infinitive form" as actual adjectives?

Good question! Simply drop the -다, and add either -ㄴ or -은.

> ### Conjugation
>
> - Verb stems ending with a vowel + -ㄴ
> - Verb stems ending with a consonant + -은

Ex)

작다 = to be small

→ 작 + -은 = 작은 = small

→ 작은 집 = a small house

빠르다 = to be fast

→ 빠르 + -ㄴ = 빠른 = fast

→ 빠른 차 = a fast car

조용하다 = to be quiet

→ 조용하 + -ㄴ = 조용한 = quiet

→ 조용한 방 = a quiet room

비싸다 = to be expensive

→ 비싸 + -ㄴ = 비싼 = expensive

→ 비싼 컴퓨터 = an expensive computer

Track 25

Exceptions

하얗다 → 하얀 = white [NOT 하얗은]

그렇다 → 그런 = such [NOT 그렇은]

달다 → 단 = sweet [NOT 달은]

* The descriptive verbs 있다 and 없다 are also an exception because they are combined with -는; this includes verbs that end in -있다 and -없다, such as 재미있다, 맛있다, 재미없다, etc.

Common Mistake

In Level 1, Lesson 5, you learned that the ending -이에요 has a similar function to "to be" in English. When it comes to using adjectives in Korean, because all adjectives are in the infinitive form already, it is INCORRECT to conjugate them with -이에요.

예쁜이에요 (×)

비싼이에요 (×)

Adjectives in the infinitive form need to be conjugated just like action verbs.

예쁘다 → 예뻐요 (○)

비싸다 → 비싸요 (○)

Sample Sentences

**Track
25**

좋은 아이디어예요.

= It is a good idea.

이상한 사람이에요.

= He is a strange person.

더 작은 가방 있어요?

= Do you have a smaller bag?

차가운 커피 마시고 싶어요.

= I want to drink some cold coffee.

나쁜 사람이에요.

= He is a bad person.

91

Sample Dialogue

A: 주연 씨, 큰 우산 있어요?

B: 아니요. 지금 비 와요?

A: 네, 많이 와요.

A: *Jooyeon, do you have a big umbrella?*

B: *No. Is it raining now?*

A: *Yes. It is raining hard.*

✏ Exercises for Lesson 13

* Review: *Change adjectives in infinitive form to adjectives with -(으)ㄴ.*

1. 작다 = to be small → (   ) = small

2. 비싸다 = to be expensive → (   ) = expensive

3. 하얗다 = to be white → (   ) = white

4. 달다 = to be sweet → (   ) = sweet

5. "To be big" is 크다 in Korean. How do you say "Do you have a bigger bag?"

(   )

Check the answers on **p.197**

by Learning Irregularities, Linking Verbs, Politeness Levels, and Much More

LESSON 14

Making Adjectives (Part 2)

Track 27

---

action verbs + -는 + 명사

You are now familiar with the fact that Korean and English have different systems when it comes to using adjectives. In the previous lesson, you learned how to create adjectives from adjectives in their infinitive form (also known as "descriptive verb form"). You will now boost your knowledge of Korean adjectives with this lesson on making adjectives from action verbs.

Adjectives are a part of speech which modify a noun or pronoun. In both Korean and English, the adjective is placed before the noun/pronoun, just as the "nice" in "nice person" or "fun" in "fun game".

In Korean, not only can adjectives in their infinitive form be used as adjectives, but action verbs can be conjugated to be used as adjectives, too!

Example of adjectives in infinitive form used as adjectives

Nice person (nice + person)

= adjective in infinitive form 좋다 + 사람 = 좋은 사람

Fun game (fun + game)

= adjective in infinitive form 재미있다 + 게임 = 재미있는 게임

Examples of action verbs used as adjectives

노래하는 사람

= 노래하다 (to sing) + 사람 (person)

= (the/a) person who sings

Track 27

좋아하는 책

= 좋아하다 (to like) + 책 (book)

= (the/a) book that I like

→ book who likes (×)

As can be seen from the examples above, when verbs are changed into adjectives, the meaning can differ depending on the context. Just remember that the adjective is somehow modifying the noun, and judging from the overall context, the meaning of the adjective should be clear.

> *Conjugation*
> Verb stem + -는

95

Ex)

가다 = to go

Adjective form: 가는

자다 = to sleep

Adjective form: 자는

For verb stems ending with ㄹ, drop ㄹ and add -는.

Ex)

열다 = to open

Adjective form: 여는

Track 27

불다 = to blow

Adjective form: 부는

The adjective in certain sentences can actually be an adjective clause (a clause which modifies a noun/pronoun).

Ex)

좋아하다 = to like; to love

Adjective form: 좋아하는

좋아하는 책 = a book that I/you/they/someone like(s)

내가/제가 좋아하는 책 = a book which I like

(**내가/제가 좋아하는** (which I like) is the adjective clause here.)

내가/제가 안 좋아하는 책 = a book that I do not like

(내가/제가 안 좋아하는 is the adjective clause here.)

좋아하는 is the adjective form of 좋아하다, and it means "which I like" or "that someone likes". Depending on the context and the use of particles, the meaning of the sentence can change.

Ex)

좋아하는 사람

= someone who someone likes

= someone I like

민지가 좋아하는 사람

= someone who Minji likes

Track 27

민지를 좋아하는 사람

= someone who likes Minji

Sample Sentences

이 노래는 제가 좋아하는 노래예요.

= This song is a song that I like.

자주 먹는 한국 음식 있어요?

= Is there a Korean food that you eat often?

자주 가는 카페 있어요?

= Is there a cafe that you go to often?

요즘 좋아하는 가수는 누구예요?

= Which singer do you like these days?

요즘 공부하고 있는 외국어는 일본어예요.

= The foreign language I am studying these days is Japanese.

눈이 오는 날에는 영화 보고 싶어요.

= On a day when it snows, I want to see a movie.

Track 27

저기 있는 사람, 아는 사람이에요?

= That person who is over there, is it someone that you know?

배고픈 사람 (있어요)?

= Anybody (who is) hungry?

Sample Dialogue

Track 28

A: 경은 씨 옷은 다 예쁜 것 같아요.

B: 고마워요.

A: 자주 가는 옷 가게가 있어요?

B: 네, 저희 집 앞에 있어요.

A: *I think your clothes are all pretty, Kyeong-eun.*

B: *Thank you.*

A: *Do you have a clothing store that you often visit?*

B: *Yes. It is in front of my house.*

by Learning Irregularities, Linking Verbs, Politeness Levels, and Much More

✏ Exercises for Lesson 14

Check the answers on **p.197**

Match the English phrase with the Korean equivalent:

1. someone I like

a. 민지를 좋아하는 사람

2. someone who Minji likes

b. 좋아하는 사람

3. someone who likes Minji

c. 민지가 좋아하는 사람

Translate the following sentences to Korean:

4. Is there a Korean food that you eat often?
* 먹다 = to eat
* 자주 = often

(   )

5. Which singer do you like these days?
* 좋아하다 = to like; to love
* 요즘 = these days

(   )

LESSON **15**

Well then, In that case, If so

그러면, 그럼

안녕하세요! Welcome back to another lesson on conjunctions! Hooray! By the end of this lesson, you will learn how to use a Korean conjunction which means "well then", "in that case", or "if so".

그러면 = in that case; if so; then

Do you remember -(으)면? Yes, that is right. It was introduced in Level 2, Lesson 23! 만약 -(으)면 or -(으)면 means "if" or "in case". 그러면 is a combination of 그렇다, which means "to be so", and -면.

A shorter version of 그러면

In spoken Korean (and often in casual written Korean), instead of saying 그러면, sometimes people use the shortened form, 그럼. Try not to confuse it with 그런, which means "such".

101

Sample Sentences

그러면 이거는 뭐예요?

= Then, what is THIS?

지금 바빠요? 그러면 언제 안 바빠요?

= You are busy now? Then WHEN are you not busy?

한국 음식 좋아해요? 그럼 김밥도 좋아해요?

= Do you like Korean food? Then do you like gimbap, too?

진짜요? 그럼 이제 어떻게 해요?

= Really? If so, what do we do now?

Track 29

그럼 이거는 어때요?

= Then how about this one?

* As an adverb, 그럼 (shortening of 그러면) indeed means "then" or "in that case". However, the interjection 그럼 (or 그럼요 in polite form) means "of course!" or "naturally!" Depending on the context you can distinguish the difference between the two.

Sample Dialogue

Track 30

A: 우체국 옆에 냉면 맛있는 집 있는 거 알아요?

B: 아니요, 몰랐어요.

A: 그럼 오늘 점심 거기서 먹을까요?

B: 네, 좋아요.

A: *Do you know that there is a good cold noodle restaurant next to the post office?*

B: *No. I didn't know that.*

A: *Then, shall we have lunch there today?*

B: *Okay. Sounds good.*

by Learning Irregularities, Linking Verbs, Politeness Levels, and Much More

✏ Exercises for Lesson 15

1. How do you say "in that case", "if so", or "well then" in Korean?

(   )

1-1. Often used in spoken Korean (and in casual written Korean), what is the shortened form of the previous answer?

(   )

Write the following sentences in Korean:

2. You're busy now? Then when are you not busy?
    * To be busy = 바쁘다

(   )

3. Then, what is THIS?

(   )

Check the answers on **p.197**

LESSON **16**

Let's

-아/어/여요 (청유형)

Track 31

안녕하세요! "Let's" get right into this lesson! When asking other people to do something with you, in English, you would most likely say something such as "Let's go", "Let's do it", or "Let's start."

There are a few different ways to say "let's" in Korean:

1. -아/어/여요 [polite/plain]
2. -(으)시죠 [honorific]
3. -자 [informal]
4. -(으)ㄹ래요? [polite/casual]
5. -(으)실래요? [polite/formal]

Ex)

시작하다 = to start; to begin

1. 시작해요. = Let's start. (plain)

2. 시작하시죠. = Let's start. (honorific)

3. 시작하자. = Let's start. (informal)

4. 시작할래요? = Shall we start? (polite/casual)

5. 시작하실래요? = Shall we start? (polite/formal)

The most frequently used form is the first example above, -아/어/여요. As the most heard and used way to say "yes", this lesson will focus only on this ending. The other forms will be covered through future lessons.

Track 31

-아/어/여요

If you are looking at this verb ending and wondering why it looks the same as the plain present tense ending, that is because it is! Although it is the exact same ending, you generally tell the difference through context. Take a look at a few sample sentences to see how easily the meaning can be determined.

Sample Sentences

저도 서점에 갈 거예요. 같이 가요!

= I'm going to the bookstore, too. Let's go together!

배 안 고파요? 우리 햄버거 먹어요.

= Aren't you hungry? Let's eat hamburgers.

지금 두 시예요. 세 시에 여기에서 만나요.

= It is two o'clock now. Let's meet here at three o'clock.

저 금요일까지 바빠요. 토요일에 시작해요. 어때요?

= I will be busy until Friday. Let's start on Saturday. What do you think?

다른 데 가요. 여기 안 좋은 것 같아요.

= Let's go somewhere else. I think this place is not so good.

* Most Korean phrase books out there will teach learners the ending -(으)ㅂ시다. There
[-(eu)p-ssi-da]

are some situations where the use of -(으)ㅂ시다 would be natural, but not in everyday

situations. For example, when talking with close friends, -(으)ㅂ시다 should never be used.

The appropriate usage of -(으)ㅂ시다 will be introduced in a future lesson, but for now,

please use -아/어/여요.

Track
31

Sample Dialogue

Track 32

A: 경화 씨, 일 시작하기 전에 저랑 잠깐 이야기 좀 해요.

B: 네, 지금 해요.

A: 좋아요. 그럼 잠깐 나갈까요?

A: Kyung-hwa, let's have a chat for a moment before you start working.

B: Sure. Let's talk now.

A: Good. Then shall we go out for a second?

✏ Exercises for Lesson 16

1. There are a few different ways to say "let us" or "let's" in Korean. What is the most frequently used way of saying "let's" in Korean?

(   )

2. Circle the form which is NOT translated as "Let's ..." in Korean:

    a. -아/어/여요   b. -(으)시죠   c. -자   d. -(으)ㄴ

3. Circle the sentence which does NOT mean "Let's start" in Korean:

    * 시작하다 = to start; to begin

    a. 시작해요.   b. 시작하자.   c. 시작하고 싶어요.   d. 시작할래요?

Fill in the blanks with the correct Korean sentence.

4. I'm going to the bookstore, too. Let's go together!

    * bookstore = 서점

    저도 서점에 갈 거예요. (   )

5. Aren't you hungry? Let's eat hamburgers.

    * hamburger = 햄버거

    배 안 고파요? (   )

Check the answers on **p.198**

109

LESSON **17**

In order to, For the sake of

위해, 위해서

Track 33

In this lesson, you will learn an expression that means "in order to", "for", or "for the sake of". The keyword in the expression is 위하다.

위하다 means "to put forth the effort for something/someone" or "to do something to benefit someone", but it is rarely used as is without being changed to another form.

위해 = **위해서** = in order to/for

위하다 is rarely used in its dictionary form, and it is changed to forms such as "위해" or "위해서" to mean "in order to", "in order for", or "for the sake of".

위해 = 위하여
위해서 = 위하여서

110

There will be times when you encounter 위하여 rather than 위해. 위하여 is the original conjugation, but in everyday language, 위하여 is shortened to 위해 (both in written and spoken languages) for the ease of pronunciation.

Using 위해/위해서 with nouns

> Noun + -을/를 위해(서)
>
> = in order for + noun = for the sake of + noun

Ex)

건강을 위해서

= for health; for the sake of health; in order to be healthy

Track 33

회사를 위해서

= for the company; for the good of the company

Using 위해/위해서 with verbs

> Verb stem + -기 위해(서)

Ex)

한국에 가기 위해서

= in order to go to Korea

일본어를 배우기 위해서

= in order to learn Japanese

* Please note that using 위해(서) in a sentence makes it sound very formal.
You will hear/see this a lot in song lyrics, books, and news articles, but not in casual, spoken conversations.

Sample Sentences

슈퍼맨은 세계 평화를 위해서 일해요.

= Superman works for world peace.

Track 33

저는 한국에 가기 위해서 열심히 공부했어요.

= I studied hard in order to go to Korea.

부모님을 위해서 돈을 모았어요.

= I saved up money for my parents.

건강을 위해서 매일 운동하고 있어요.

= I am exercising every day for my health.

Sample Dialogue

Track 34

A: 유럽으로 배낭여행을 가기 위해서 돈을 모으고 있어요.

B: 우와! 언제 갈 거예요?

A: 이번 여름 방학 때 갈 거예요.

A: I am saving up money to go backpacking in Europe.

B: Wow! When are you going to go?

A: I am going to go during this summer vacation.

113

✏ *Exercises for Lesson* 17

1. How do you say "in order to", "for", or "for the sake of" in Korean?

( )

2. How do you write "for health", "for the sake of health", or "in order to be healthy"?
* health = 건강

( )

3. Write "in order to go to Korea" in Korean.
* to go = 가다

( )

Check the answers on **p.198**

4. Translate "I studied hard in order to go to Korea" to Korean.
* to study = 공부하다

( )

5. Write the following sentence in Korean: "I am exercising everyday for my health."
* to exercise = 운동하다

( )

Expand Your Knowledge of Korean

LESSON **18**

Nothing but, Only

-밖에 + 부정형

Track 35

In Level 2, Lesson 15, you learned how to use -만 with nouns, pronouns, or noun forms of verbs. The expression introduced in this lesson can only be used with negative verb conjugations and consists of two parts: -밖에 + negative verb conjugation.

The way this works is similar to saying "nothing else but" or "do not do anything other than" in English.

밖 = outside; outdoors

밖에 = outside something; other than something; out of the range of something

-밖에 + negative verb conjugation = ONLY + verb

> ### *Conjugation*
> Noun + **-밖에** + negative conjugation

Ex)

콜라(를) 마시다 = to drink cola

콜라밖에 안 마시다 = to only drink cola

돈(이) 있다 = to have money

돈(이) 없다 = to not have money

돈밖에 없다 = to have nothing but money, to only have money

> *Q : Are -만 and -밖에 interchangeable?*
>
> *A : The answer is yes and no. Sometimes they are interchangeable, but you have to change the verb to a negative form when using -밖에. -밖에 is generally used more than -만.*

-밖에 cannot be used with imperative sentences (sentences which request something or give instructions) including -아/어/여 주세요 ("do something for me"), so -만 must be used instead (i.e. 이것만 주세요 = Give me this one only).

In addition, when the verb itself has a negative meaning, -만 is more commonly used than -밖에 (i.e. 저는 닭고기만 싫어해요 = I only hate chicken).

Sample Sentences

한국인 친구가 한 명밖에 없어요.

= I only have one Korean friend.

116

한국인 친구는 한 명밖에 없어요.

= As for Korean friends, I only have one.

한국어 조금밖에 못 해요.

= I can only speak a little bit of Korean.

   * Please note that this is not "한국어 조금만 할 수 있어요. (I can speak a little bit of

   Korean.)" Although you will be understood if you say this, to sound more natural,

   please say "한국어 조금밖에 못 해요."

이것밖에 없어요?

= This is it?

= You only have this?

Track
35

우리 고양이는 참치밖에 안 먹어요.

= My cat only eats tuna.

왜 공부밖에 안 해요?

= Why do you only study?

= Why do you do nothing but study?

117

Sample Dialogue

Track 36

A: 민석 씨, 어제 생일 파티에 몇 명 왔어요?

B: 별로 안 왔어요.

A: 몇 명 정도 왔어요?

B: 백 명밖에 안 왔어요.

A: Minseok, how many people came to your birthday party yesterday?

B: Not many people came.

A: About how many people came?

B: Only 100 people came.

✎ Exercises for Lesson 18

Match the English phrase with its Korean equivalent:

1. To have nothing but money; to only have money

a. 돈(이) 없다

2. To have money

b. 돈밖에 없다

3. To not have money

c. 돈(이) 있다

Check the answers on **p.198**

Write the following sentences in Korean:

4. As for Korean friends, I only have one.
  * 한국인 친구 = Korean friend

(   )

5. I can only speak a little bit of Korean.

(   )

119

LESSON **19**

After -ing

다음에, 후에, 뒤에

Track 37

There are a few different ways to say "after -ing" in Korean, and through this lesson, you will learn the three most common ways to say it. These three expressions all share a common structure:

-(으)ㄴ + 다음에

-(으)ㄴ + 후에

-(으)ㄴ + 뒤에

These three mean "after -ing", but each of the key nouns have a different meaning.

다음 = next time; next
(i.e. 다음 주 = next week)

120

후 = after

(i.e. 오후 = afternoon)

뒤 = behind; back

(i.e. 등 뒤 = behind the back)

As standalone words, the meanings are quite different, right? However, you can use any of these three words to create a sentence which means "After -ing". These three expressions are interchangeable, and the meaning does not change no matter which noun is used.

Conjugation

Verb stem + -(으)ㄴ + 다음(or 후/뒤)에 = after -ing

In Lessons 13 and 14, you learned how to conjugate verbs into adjectives using -(으)ㄴ. Here, -(으)ㄴ indicates that the verb was done in the past, which makes the adjective clause "after -ing" past tense.

Ex)

편지를 받다 = to receive a letter

편지를 받은 다음에 = after receiving a letter

편지를 받은 후에 = after receiving a letter

편지를 받은 뒤에 = after receiving a letter

집에 가다 = to go home

집에 간 다음에 = after going home

집에 간 후에 = after going home

121

집에 간 뒤에 = after going home

책을 읽다 = to read a book

책을 읽은 다음에 = after reading a book

책을 읽은 후에 = after reading a book

책을 읽은 뒤에 = after reading a book

Sample Sentences

영화 본 다음에 우리 커피 마셔요.

= After watching the movie, let's drink coffee.

Track 37

점심을 먹은 다음에, 도서관에 갔어요.

= After having lunch, I went to the library.

이거 한 다음에 뭐 할 거예요?

= After doing this, what are you going to do?

그거요? 이거 한 뒤에 할게요.

= That one? I will do it after I do this.

결정한 후에 연락 주세요.

= Contact me after you decide.

Sample Dialogue

A: 현우 씨가 지금 녹음실 쓰고 있어요?

B: 네.

A: 그럼 현우 씨 쓴 다음에 제가 쓸게요.

A: Is Hyunwoo using the recording room now?

B: Yes.

A: Then I will use it after he is finished.

Track 38

by Learning Irregularities, Linking Verbs, Politeness Levels, and Much More

✎ Exercises for Lesson 19

Check the answers on **p.198**

Translate the following clauses and sentences to Korean:

1. After receiving a letter

  * to receive a letter = 편지를 받다

  (   )

2. After reading a book

  * to read a book = 책을 읽다

  (   )

3. After watching the movie, let's drink coffee.

  * to watch a movie = 영화 보다   ** to drink coffee = 커피 마시다

  (   )

4. Contact me after you decide.

  * to decide = 결정하다

  (   )

5. After doing this, what are you going to do?

  (   )

LESSON 20

Even if, Even though

-아/어/여도

In Level 3, Lesson 12, you were introduced to the conjunction 그래도, which means "but still" or "nevertheless" and is generally used to begin a sentence. The verb ending in this lesson has the same meaning as 그래도, but it is used as a subordinating conjunction (joins the main clause to the dependent clause) to combine two sentences without having to end one sentence and begin another.

-아/어/여도 = even if, even though

Conjugation

Verb stems ending with the vowel ㅗ or ㅏ + -아도

Verb stems ending with other vowels + -어도

Verb stems ending with 하 + -여도

Ex)

보다 = to see

→ 보아도 = 봐도 = even if you see; even if you look

울다 = to cry

→ 울어도 = even if you cry; even though you cry

공부하다 = to study

→ 공부해도 (= 공부하여도) = even if you study; even though you study

Combining two sentences together:

Track 39

요즘에 바빠요. + 그래도 운동은 하고 있어요.

= I am busy these days. But still, I am doing some exercise.

→ 요즘에 바빠도, 운동은 하고 있어요.

= Even though I am busy these days, I am still doing some exercise.

Sample Sentences

집에 가도, 밥이 없어요.

= Even if I go home, there is no food.

택시를 타도, 시간이 오래 걸려요.

= It takes a long time even if I take a taxi.

석진 씨는 제가 전화를 해도 안 받아요.

= Even if I call him, Seokjin does not answer.

냄새는 이상해도 맛있어요.

= It is tasty even though it smells weird.

바빠도 한국에 갈 거예요.

= Even if I am busy, I will go to Korea.

Track 39

127

Sample Dialogue

 Track 40

A: 경화 씨한테 계속 전화를 해도
안 받아요.

B: 자고 있는 거 아닐까요?

A: 아직도요?

A: *Kyung-hwa is not answering even though I keep calling her.*

B: *Maybe she is still in bed?*

A: *Still?*

✎ Exercises for Lesson **20**

Write the following phrases or sentences in Korean:

1. Even if you cry; even though you cry
  * 울다 = to cry

  (   )

2. Even if you study; even though you study

  (   )

3. Even if you see; even if you look
  * 보다 = to see

  (   )

4. It takes a long time even if I take a taxi.
  * 택시를 타다 = to take a taxi

  (   )

5. Even if I go home, there is no food.
  * 집에 가다 = to go home

  (   )

Check the answers on **p.198**

BLOG

BOARD GAME CAFES
(보드 게임 카페)

Finding ways to entertain or pass the time with your 친구 (friends) and 가족 (family) in Korea isn't very difficult, especially with the multitude of 방 (rooms) on every street that are there for just that purpose. A 노래방, or "singing room", is a super popular choice of entertainment for everyone no matter what age or time of day. A PC방 is where you and your friends can play PC games to your heart's content for a small hourly fee. A DVD방 is smaller and more intimate than a 영화관 (movie theater) as it includes a huge collection of movies to choose from and is a private room which includes a couch, wide-screen TV, and surround sound. Then there is the 보드 카페 or 보드 게임 카페 or 보드 카페 게임방⋯ whatever you choose to call it, it translates to English as "board game cafe/room".

Although the 보드 카페 fad peaked about 10 years ago, you can still find a good number of these cafes around town, especially in places where the nightlife is really hoppin' (typically around universities.) In Seoul, these areas include 홍대, 강남, 명동, 신촌, 압구정⋯etc.

131

At the 보드 카페, you can spend as much time playing your favorite board games as your money will permit. For just 1,000-2,000원 per person for an hour, you and your friends choose an empty table, then a waitress/waiter will come and bring you the menu of games! 4-6 people per table works the best, but you can choose from a ton of games, including Risk, Life, MadGab, Clue, UNO, Battleship, SORRY!...the list seriously seems like it goes on forever. After the game is chosen, tell your waitress/waiter your choice and he/she will bring the game to your table. The 직원/종업원 (employees) are well-versed on how to play all of the games, so if there are any questions or discrepancies in how a game is played, just call over your waiter/waitress and he/she will explain it to you. If you're in the middle of a game and become bored, or someone is getting too intense and frustrated (everyone has that friend or family member⋯), you can switch games. In fact, you can switch as many times as you'd like!

In addition to board games, you can also purchase 음료 (drinks) and 과자/스낵 (snacks). After all, it is a cafe, so what good would it be if you couldn't order coffee? Most 보드 카페 places will not say anything if you decide to bring your own refreshments.

Oh yeah! I forgot to mention that if someone loses, you get to use one of those giant squeaky plastic hammers to whack the loser on the head. :D

Korea's 보드 카페: just one of the many ways to cure boredom and have some fun with your friends or family while you're here.

You're almost finished with Level 3!

Keep up the good work!

화이팅~

LESSON 21

Linking Verbs

-는/은/ㄴ데

Track 41

The verb ending in this lesson has an incredibly versatile meaning. While the basic structure ends in -데, the words or phrases which come right before -데 change a bit.

Conjugation

1. -는데 is used after action verbs, after 있다 and 없다, and after -았 or -겠.

2. -은데 is used after descriptive verbs which have a final consonant in the verb stem, except for the consonant ㄹ.

3. -ㄴ데 is used after descriptive verbs which end in a vowel or the consonant ㄹ (in this case, ㄹ is dropped), and after 이다 and 아니다.

Ex)

하다 → 하는데

있다 → 있는데

먹다 → 먹는데

작다 → 작은데

좁다 → 좁은데

예쁘다 → 예쁜데

멀다 → 먼데

Variety of Usage

The way this ending can be used is very diverse.

Track 41

Usage 1

Explaining the background or the situation before making a suggestion, a request, or a question.

Ex)

내일 일요일인데, 뭐 할 거예요?

= It is Sunday tomorrow + (-ㄴ데) + what are you going to do?

Usage 2

Explaining the situation first before explaining what happened.

Ex)

어제 자고 있었는데, 한국에서 전화가 왔어요.

= I was sleeping yesterday + (-는데) + I got a phone call from Korea.

Usage 3

Showing a result or situation which is contrasting to the previous action or situation.

Ex)

아직 9시인데 벌써 졸려요.

= It is still 9 o'clock but I am already sleepy.

The second part (after -는데) can be omitted when the meaning is easily implied.

Ex)

준비 많이 했는데(요)...

= I prepared a lot, but...

Track
41

Usage 4

Showing surprise or exclamation.

Ex)

멋있는데(요)!

= Oh, that is cool!

Usage 5

Asking a question (expecting some explanation about a situation or behavior).

Ex)

지금 어디에 있는데(요)?

= So where are you now?

Usage 6

Expecting an answer or a response.

Ex)

지금(요)? 지금 바쁜데(요).

= Now? I am busy now, so...

Sample Sentences

내일 친구 생일인데, 선물을 아직 못 샀어요.

= It is my friend's birthday tomorrow, but I have not been able to buy a present.

이거 일본에서 샀는데, 선물이에요.

= I bought this in Japan, and it is a present for you.

Track 41

오늘 뉴스에서 봤는데, 그거 진짜예요?

= I saw it in the news today. Is that for real?

이거 좋은데요!

= I like this! / This is good!

어? 여기 있었는데.

= Huh? It was here...

영화 재미있었는데, 무서웠어요.

= The movie was interesting, but it was scary.

137

영화 봤는데, 무서웠어요.

= I saw a movie, and it was scary.

저 지금 학생인데, 일도 하고 있어요.

= I am a student now, but I am working, too.

Track 41

Sample Dialogue

Track
42

A: 이 가방 너무 사고 싶어요.

B: 사세요. 지금 세일하지 않아요?

A: 맞아요. 지금 세일하고 있는데, 세일해도 너무 비싸요.

A: *I want to buy this bag so bad.*

B: *Buy it. Isn't it on sale now?*

A: *Right. It is on sale now, but it is still too expensive.*

Check the answers on **p.198**

✎ Exercises for Lesson 21

1. "Sunday" is "일요일" in Korean. How do you say "It's Sunday tomorrow + (-ㄴ데) + what are you going to do?" (explaining the background or the situation before making a suggestion, a request, or a question).

(   )

2. "To get a phone call" is "전화가 오다" in Korean. How do you write "I was sleeping yesterday + (-는데) + I got a phone call from Korea." (explaining the situation before explaining what happened)?

(   )

3. "To be scary" is "무섭다" in Korean. How do you say "I saw a movie, and it was scary"?

(   )

4. "The news" is "뉴스" in Korean. How do you write "I saw it in the news today. Is that for real?"

(   )

5. How do you say "I like this! / This is good!" (showing surprise or exclamation)?

(   )

LESSON 22

Maybe I might…

-(으)ㄹ 수도 있어요

In this lesson, you will learn about the expression **-(으)ㄹ 수도 있다**. This is a combination of two grammar points which were covered in previous lessons:

Track
43

1. -(으)ㄹ 수 있다 was introduced in Level 2, Lesson 17, and it means "can, to be able to".
2. -도 was introduced in Level 2, Lesson 13, and it means "also, too".

When these two expressions are combined into -(으)ㄹ 수도 있다, it means "it could…", "it is possible that…", or "it might…". In order to understand why -(으)ㄹ 수도 있다 has such meanings, you first need to take a closer look at the expression -(으)ㄹ 수 있다.

Basically, the word 수 is a noun which, in this particular structure, means "way", "method", or "idea". Therefore, -(으)ㄹ 수 있다 means "there is a way to do…", "there is an idea for doing…", or "there is a possibility for doing…".

141

When the meaning of -도, which is "also" or "too", is added to -(으)ㄹ 수 있다, the sentence takes the meaning of "there is also the possibility of...".

Although -(으)ㄹ 수도 있다 COULD mean "to also be able to do something", it usually means "it might", "it could", or "perhaps".

Ex)

알다 = to know (something/someone)

→ 알 수도 있다 = might know (something/someone)

→ 제 친구가 알 수도 있어요. = My friend might know (the person/the thing).

만나다 = to meet

→ 만날 수도 있다 = might meet

→ 내일 다시 만날 수도 있어요. = We might meet again tomorrow.

작다 = to be small

→ 작을 수도 있다 = might be small

→ 모자가 작을 수도 있어요. = The hat could be small.

Sample Sentences

저 내일 올 수도 있어요.

= I might come here tomorrow.

저 내일 안 올 수도 있어요.

= I might not come here tomorrow.

142

저 내일 못 올 수도 있어요.

= I might not be able to come here tomorrow.

이거 가짜일 수도 있어요.

= This might be fake.

정말 그럴 수도 있어요.

= It might really be so.

Track
43

by Learning Irregularities, Linking Verbs, Politeness Levels, and Much More

Sample Dialogue

Track
44

A: 저 다음 달에 일본 갈 수도 있어요.

B: 아, 진짜요? 오세요. 오세요.

A: 그런데 확실한 것은 아니에요.
   안 갈 수도 있어요.

A: I might go to Japan next month.

B: Oh, really? Come! Come!

A: But, I am not sure yet. I might not go.

144

✏ Exercises for Lesson 22

Write the following words and/or phrases in Korean:

1. Might know (something or someone)
   * To know = 알다

   (   )

2. Might meet
   * To meet = 만나다

   (   )

3. Might be small
   * To be small = 작다

   (   )

4. I might come here tomorrow.
   * To come = 오다

   (   )

5. This might be fake.
   * To be fake = 가짜이다

   (   )

Check the answers on **p.198**

145

LESSON 23

Word Builder 1

학(學)

Track 45

Welcome to the first Word Builder lesson of Talk To Me In Korean! Word Builder lessons are designed to help you understand how to more efficiently expand your vocabulary by learning/understanding some common and basic building blocks of Korean words. Many (not all) of the words and letters introduced through Word Builder lessons are based on Chinese characters, or 한자, but the meanings can differ from modern-day Chinese. Your goal, through these lessons, is to understand how words are formed and remember the keywords in Korean in order to expand your Korean vocabulary from there. You certainly do not have to memorize the Hanja characters, but if you want to, feel free!

Today's keyword is 학.

The Chinese character for this word is 學.

The word 학 is related to "learning", "studying", and "school".

146

Sample Expressions

학 + 생 (person, member, participant) = 학생 (學生) = student

학 + 교 (school) = 학교 (學校) = school

학 + 원 (house; garden) = 학원 (學院) = private academy

수 (numbers) + 학 = 수학 (數學) = mathematics

과 (subject; class; species) + 학 = 과학 (科學) = science

어 (word) + 학 = 어학 (語學) = language learning

언어 (word + word) + 학 = 언어학 (言語學) = linguistics

경제 (economy) + 학 = 경제학 (經濟學) = economics

학 + 자 (person) = 학자 (學者) = scholar

Track 45

유 (to stay) + 학 = 유학 (留學) = studying abroad; staying abroad to study

유학 (studying abroad) + 생 = 유학생 (留學生) = student studying abroad

전 (to roll, move) + 학 = 전학 (轉學) = to change schools

전학 (to change schools) + 생 = 전학생 (轉學生) = student who moved to another school

학 + 년 (year) = 학년 (學年) = school year

학 + 기 (period) = 학기 (學期) = semester

방 (to release, let go) + 학 = 방학 (放學) = school vacation

장 (recommending) + 학 + 금 (money) = 장학금 (獎學金) = scholarship

장 + 학 + 생 = 장학생 (獎學生) = student on a scholarship

복 (return) + 학 + 생 = 복학생 (復學生)

= student who has returned to school (usually) after a long break

학 + 습 (acquire) = 학습 (學習) = (formal) learning, studies

한국어 학습 (韓國語 學習) = (formal) Korean learning

독 (alone) + 학 = 독학 (獨學) = self-study, studying by oneself

Track 45

Sample Dialogue

Track
46

A: 저 드라마 저희 학교에서 찍고
  있어요.

B: 진짜요? 언제 찍어요?

A: 학생들 없는 일요일에 찍어요.

A: *That drama is set in my school.*

B: *Really? When do they film?*

A: *They film on Sundays when there are
  no students.*

149

✎ Exercises for Lesson 23

1. The word $\Big($ $\Big)$ is related to "learning", "studying", and "school".

Write the following words in Korean. All given words are Sino-Korean.

Check the answers on **p.198**

2. Changing schools
   * 전 (轉) = to move; to roll

(   )

3. Scholarship
   * 장 (獎) = recommend

(   )

4. Mathematics
   * 수 (數) = numbers

(   )

5. School year
   * 년 (年) = year

(   )

LESSON **24**

Irregulars: 르

르 불규칙

Welcome to another lesson on irregularities. Yay! You will learn about irregular 르 in this lesson, which occurs more often than you think. Are you ready? 시작!

Track 47

Irregular 르 is applied only on the following three occasions as follows.

Verb stems ending with -르 followed by:
1. -아/어/여요
2. -아/어/여서
3. -았/었/였어요

In these cases, 르 is changed to ㄹ and placed at the end of the previous vowel. ONE MORE ㄹ is needed before adding the verb ending.

Even if the verb stem ends with -르, if it is then followed by other endings, such as -고, -는데, etc., -르 will still stay the same.

151

Ex)

고르다 = to choose; to pick; to select

→ 골라요. = I pick.

→ 골라서 = I pick and then; because I pick

→ 골랐어요. = I picked.

모르다 = to not know

→ 몰라요. = I do not know.

→ 몰라서 = because I do not know

→ 몰랐어요. = I did not know.

빠르다 = to be fast

→ 빨라요. = It is fast.

Track 47

→ 빨라서 = because it is fast

→ 빨랐어요. = It was fast.

자르다 = to cut

→ 잘라요. = I cut.

→ 잘라서 = I cut and then; because I cut

→ 잘랐어요. = I cut.

기르다 = to grow, to raise

→ 길러요. = I raise.

→ 길러서 = I raise and then; because I raise

→ 길렀어요. = I raised.

Sample Sentences

뭐 골랐어요?

= What did you choose?

저도 몰라요.

= I do not know, either.

비행기는 빨라서 좋아요.

= Planes are good because they are fast. / I like airplanes because they are fast.

누가 케이크 잘랐어요?

= Who cut the cake?

Track 47

토끼를 5년 동안 길렀어요.

= I had a rabbit as a pet for five years. / I raised a rabbit for five years.

by Learning Irregularities, Linking Verbs, Politeness Levels, and Much More

Sample Dialogue

A: 주연 씨, 마시고 싶은 거 골랐어요?

B: 아니요, 아직 안 골랐어요.

A: 빨리 고르세요.

A: *Jooyeon, have you chosen what you would like to drink?*

B: *No. I have not chosen yet.*

A: *Please hurry up.*

✎ Exercises for Lesson 24

Translate the following to Korean:

1. [Past tense] I picked (it).
   * 고르다 = to pick; to select

   (   )

2. What did you choose?

   (   )

3. [Past tense] I cut (it).
   * 자르다 = to cut

   (   )

4. Who cut the cake?

   (   )

5. Planes are good because they are fast.
   * 빠르다 = to be fast

   (   )

Check the answers on **p.199**

155

LESSON **25**

Verb Ending

-네요

Track 49

As you have learned so far, there are many different types of verb endings in Korean, each of which have very specific rules. This one is no exception. Changing a plain sentence to end with **-네요** expresses that you are impressed, surprised, or your own personal thought. This ending is used quite frequently in everyday Korean conversation as well as in Korean dramas.

For example, saying "맛있어요" just means "it is delicious." Saying "맛있네요", on the other hand, expresses that you are impressed or surprised by the taste. While "맛있어요" can mean the same thing when said with the right intonation, it cannot convey the same message when it is written.

> ### *Conjugation*
> Verb stem + -네요
> -었/았/였 (past tense suffix) + -네요

Ex)

크다 = to be big (verb stem = 크)

크 + 어요 → 커요. = It is big. (Fact)

크 + 네요 → 크네요. = (I see that) it is big. / (Oh, I did not know it was big, but) it is big. (Expressing surprise)

잘 어울리다 = to suit someone well; to go well with someone

잘 어울리 + 어요 → 잘 어울려요. = It looks good on you. (Fact)

잘 어울리 + 네요 → 잘 어울리네요. = Oh! I find that it looks good on you. (Expressing your impression)

맞다 = to be correct

맞 + 아요 → 맞아요. = It is correct. (Fact)

맞 + 네요 → 맞네요. = I see that it is correct! (Finding out a fact for the first time.)

Track 49

Sample Sentences

여기 있네요!

= Oh, here it is!

이 드라마 재미있네요.

= I find this drama fun to watch.

　* If you already know that this drama is fun and you are telling someone else that as a fact, you need to say "이 드라마 재미있어요."

157

별로 안 춥네요.

= Well, it is not that cold.

아무도 안 왔네요.

= Oh, look. Nobody is here yet.

벌써 11월이네요.

= Wow, it is already November!

Track 49

Sample Dialogue

Track 50

A: 집안일 하는 거 힘들지 않아요?

B: 힘들어요. 그래도 남편이 많이 도와줘요.

A: 오, 그래요? 좋은 남편이네요.

A: Isn't it hard to do housework?

B: It is hard, but my husband helps me a lot.

A: Oh, does he? He is a good husband!

by Learning Irregularities, Linking Verbs, Politeness Levels, and Much More

✏ Exercises for Lesson 25

Write the following expressions in Korean:

1. Oh! It looks good on you. (Expressing that you are impressed.)
   * to suit someone well = 잘 어울리다

   (   )

2. I see that it's correct! (Finding out a fact for the first time.)
   * To be correct = 맞다

   (   )

3. Oh, here it is.
   * Here = 여기

   (   )

4. Well, it's not that cold.
   * To be cold = 춥다

   (   )

5. Wow, it's already November.
   * November = 11월

   (   )

LESSON 26

Irregulars: ㄷ

ㄷ 불규칙

Track 51

You are not finished learning about irregulars yet, so get ready for a lesson on irregularities that happen with ㄷ!

How Irregular ㄷ works

When the Korean letter ㄷ is the 받침 (the final consonant at the end of a syllable) of a verb stem and is followed by a vowel, ㄷ is changed to ㄹ. Some verbs follow this rule, and some do not.

Examples of Irregular ㄷ verbs

- 듣다 = to listen
- 걷다 = to walk

- 묻다 = to ask

- 싣다 = to load

- 깨닫다 = to realize

For these verbs, ㄷ changes to ㄹ when followed by a vowel:

- 듣 + 어서 → 들어서

- 걷 + 어요 → 걸어요

- 묻 + 으면 → 물으면

- 싣 + 을 거예요 → 실을 거예요

- 깨닫 + 았어요 → 깨달았어요

Examples of verbs which do NOT follow this rule:

- 받다 = to receive

- 묻다 = to bury

- 닫다 = to close

- 믿다 = to believe

For these verbs, keep the 받침 as ㄷ, even when it is followed by a vowel:

- 받 + 아서 = 받아서

- 묻 + 어요 = 묻어요

- 닫 + 으면 = 닫으면

- 믿 + 어요 = 믿어요

* Although 묻다 (to ask) and 묻다 (to bury) are spelled the same way, they are conjugated differently and the meaning can only be determined from the context of the sentence.

Ex)

I ask. = 물어요.

I bury. = 묻어요.

Usage examples of irregular ㄷ verbs

1.

듣다 = to listen

→ 듣고 있어요

= I am listening. (ㄷ does not change because -고 begins with a consonant.)

→ 들었어요

= I heard. (ㄷ changes to ㄹ because -었 starts with a vowel.)

Track 51

2.

걷다 = to walk

→ 걷는 것 좋아해요

= I like walking. (ㄷ does not change because -는 starts with a consonant.)

→ 한 시간 걸었어요

= I walked for an hour. (ㄷ changes to ㄹ because -었 starts with a vowel.)

Sample Sentences

어디에서 들었어요?

= Where did you hear that?

많이 걸었는데, 안 피곤해요.

= I walked a lot, but I am not tired.

그 이야기를 믿어요?

= Do you believe that story?

물어도 대답이 없어요.

= Even if I ask, there is no answer.

Track 51

Sample Dialogue

Track 52

A: 방금 소리 들었어요?

B: 무슨 소리요?

A: 이상한 소리 못 들었어요?

B: 네, 못 들었어요.

A: *Did you hear that noise?*

B: *What noise?*

A: *You didn't hear the weird noise?*

B: *No, I did not.*

by Learning Irregularities, Linking Verbs, Politeness Levels, and Much More

✏ Exercises for Lesson **26**

Match the Korean word with the proper conjugation:

1. 듣다 = to listen → 듣 + 어서

2. 걷다 = to walk → 걷 + 어요

3. 받다 = to receive → 받 + 아서

4. 닫다 = to close → 닫 + 으면

5. 깨닫다 = to realize → 깨닫 + 았어요

a. 발아서
b. 받아서
c. 달으면
d. 닫으면
e. 걷어요
f. 걸어요
g. 깨닫았어요
h. 깨달았어요
i. 들어서
j. 듣어서

Check the answers on **p.199**

6. Write the following sentence in Korean: "Where did you hear that?"
   * 듣다 = to hear

   (   )

166

LESSON 27

Politeness Levels

반말 and 존댓말

Track 53

In Level 1, Lesson 1, you learned the basics of the two main categories of honorifics used in Korean. All of what you have learned so far in the Talk To Me In Korean series has been in 존댓말 (polite/formal language). In this lesson, you will learn about the casual/informal/intimate way of speaking, 반말.

Politeness levels are determined by the verb ending. There are three basic verb endings used to express different politeness levels:

Type 1. -ㅂ니다 = the most polite and most formal ending

Type 2. -(아/어/여)요 = the polite, natural, and slightly formal ending

Type 3. -아/어/여 = the casual, informal, and intimate ending

Types 1 and 2 fall under the 존댓말 category, and Type 3 goes into the 반말 category.

167

When do you use 반말?

Generally, 반말 is considered to be the most intimate and casual way of speaking with others in Korean; it has no formality at all. You can only use 반말 to someone who is younger than you, someone of the same age as you, or (if the other person is older than you) someone with whom you agreed to mutually use 반말.

If the other person's age or social status is not known, do not use 반말 in any circumstance. Once you know the other person's age and find out if he or she is younger than you, you can use 반말. However, it is safer, as well as a nice gesture, to ask the person with whom you are speaking to whether you can use 반말 with him/her.

Track 53

Common cases where 반말 is appropriate

1. You are much older than the other person and you know for sure that the other person will not be offended if you use 반말.

2. You are older than the other person, and you got his or her permission to use 반말.

3. You are of the same age as the other person, and you got his or her permission to use 반말.

4. You are in elementary school, middle school, or high school, and you know that all your classmates are of the same age as you.

5. You are talking to yourself or writing in a diary/journal.

* Remember in Korean, unlike some other cultures, it is standard etiquette to establish a speaker's position by asking one's age on first encounter. So do not be too surprised if you are asked how old you are, and use this as a tool to gauge which form of language to use. When in doubt, ALWAYS use 존댓말.

Common cases in which NOT to use 반말

1. You know the other person only through work and not personally.
2. You are older than the other person, but he or she is your business client or customer.
3. You are older than the other person, but you are talking to the person in an official environment such as business meetings, seminars, lessons, etc.
4. You do not know the other person. You just met him/her.
5. You are younger than the other person, and you never got permission from him/her that you can use 반말 to him/her.
6. You are the same age as the other person, but you are both adults, and you do not know each other that well.
7. You are older than the other person, but he/she is your boss.
8. You are older than the other person, but he or she is the spouse of your older sibling.
9. You are talking to a large group of people or filming a video blog.

Track 53

How do you ask for and give permission to speak in 반말?

There are certain expressions which people say to get permission from the other person to use 반말.

If you are the older one:

   1. 말 놔도 돼요?
   = May I speak in 반말 with you?
      * 말을 놓다 literally means to "put down the language" or "lower the language".

2. 말 편하게 해도 돼요?

= May I speak comfortably with you?

If you are the younger one:

1. 말 놓으셔도 돼요.

= You can speak casually with me.

2. 말 편하게 하셔도 돼요.

= You can speak comfortably with me. / You can speak 반말 with me.

If you are of the same age as the other person:

1. 우리 말 놓을까요?

= Shall we speak in 반말 to each other?

2. 말 편하게 해도 되죠?

= I can talk in 반말 with you, right?

How to change 존댓말 to 반말

> **Present tense**
> -아/어/여요 → -아/어/여
> -이에요 / -예요 → -이야 / -야

Ex)

What is this?

존댓말: 이거 뭐예요?

반말: 이거 뭐야?

Past tense

-았/었/였어요 → -았/었/였어

Ex)

I met a friend yesterday.

존댓말: 어제 친구 만났어요.

반말: 어제 친구 만났어.

Track 53

Future tense

-(으)ㄹ 거예요 → -(으)ㄹ 거야

Ex)

I am going to work tomorrow.

존댓말: 내일 일할 거예요.

반말: 내일 일할 거야.

Addressing people

When politely addressing someone using 존댓말, add the word 씨, as in 경은 씨, 현우 씨, 석진 씨, 소연 씨, and 현정 씨. If in a business or school setting, add the title of the person's job or status after his/her name, such as 경은 선생님, 현우 회장님, etc., to show more

171

formality toward the addressee.

When speaking in 반말, however, you can just say the name of the person without 씨. In order to make the name sound more natural when addressing the other person, add 아 or 야 to the end of the name. Names which end WITHOUT a consonant are followed by 야, and names which end WITH a consonant are followed by 아.

Ex)
경은 → 경은아! (Hey Kyeong-eun!)
현우 → 현우야! (Hey Hyunwoo!)

Speaking in Third Person

Track
53

When using a person's name while speaking or writing in third person, 이 is added after names which end with a consonant. Therefore, names such as 경은 and 석진 are followed by 이.

If 현우 wants to talk about Seokjin in a sentence, he says Seokjin's name as "석진이".

Ex)
석진이가 했어. = Seokjin did it.

Sample Dialogue

Track
54

A: 냉장고에 아이스크림 있어, 석진아.

B: 방금 밥 먹어서 배불러요.

A: 그럼 이따가 먹어.

B: 네.

A: Seokjin, there is ice cream in the refrigerator.

B: I am full because I just had a meal.

A: Then, eat it later.

B: Okay.

by Learning Irregularities, Linking Verbs, Politeness Levels, and Much More

✏️ *Exercises for Lesson **27***

Please change the following statements from **존댓말** *(polite/formal language) to* **반말** *(casual language), and write the English translation.*

1. 안녕하세요.

Casual language : ....

English translation : ....

2. 이거 뭐예요?

Casual language : ....

English translation : ....

3. 어제 친구 만났어요.

Casual language : ....

English translation : ....

True or false:

4. If you want to use **반말** (casual language) to people, you usually have to get permission.

    a. True   b. False

5. If you are older than the other person, you can use **반말** (casual language) even though you just met him/her.

    a. True   b. False

LESSON 28

"Let's" in Casual Language

-자 (반말, 청유형)

Track
55

Since you now know how and when to use 반말 (casual language), you are now well-equipped to learn how to make imperative "let us" or "let's" sentences in 반말.

Normally, for sentences in present and past tense, the suffix -요 would be dropped in order to change it from 존댓말 to 반말. When saying "let's" in 반말 however, a completely different ending is needed.

> **Conjugation**
> Verb stem + -자

Ex)

하다 = to do

하 + 자 = 하자 = Let's do it.

175

공부하다 = to study

공부하 + 자 = 공부하자 = Let's study.

하지 말다 = to not do it

하지 말 + 자 = 하지 말자 = Let's not do it.

먹다 = to eat

먹 + 자 = 먹자 = Let's eat.

Sample Sentences

Track 55

내일 보자.

= Let's meet tomorrow.

= See you tomorrow.

이거 사자.

= Let's buy this.

우리 내일은 쉬자.

= Let's take a day off tomorrow.

같이 가자.

= Let's go together.

조금만 더 기다리자.

= Let's wait a little longer.

176

More Phrases in 반말

1. 안녕하세요 → 안녕

2. 안녕히 가세요 → 안녕 / 잘 가

3. 안녕히 계세요 → 안녕 / 잘 있어

4. 저 → 나

5. ~ 씨 / You → 너

6. 네 / 예 → 응 / 어

Track 55

7. 아니요 → 아니 / 아니야

Sample Dialogue

🎙️ Track 56

A: 밥 먹자. 배고파.

B: 뭐 먹을까?

A: 중국 음식 먹을까?

B: 그래.

A: Let's eat! I am hungry.

B: What shall we eat?

A: Shall we have Chinese food?

B: Sure.

✏ *Exercises for Lesson 28*

Write the following phrases in Korean using 반말 *(casual language):*

1. Let's do it.
  * To do = 하다

(   )

2. Let's not do it.
  * To not do (something) = 하지 말다

(   )

3. Let's buy this.
  * To buy = 사다

(   )

4. Let's wait a little longer.
  * To wait = 기다리다

(   )

5. Let's go together.
  * To go = 가다

(   )

Check the answers on **p.199**

179

LESSON 29

Irregulars: ㅅ

ㅅ 불규칙

Track 57

Do you remember the previous lessons in this book over irregularities with ㅂ, 르, and ㄷ? Of course you do! Now that you have become a master of irregularities, learning "Irregular ㅅ" will be no match for you!

When ㅅ is the 받침 of a verb stem and it is followed by a vowel, the ㅅ is dropped.

Ex)

낫다 = to heal; to recover; to be better (in comparison)

낫 + 아요 (present tense) → 나아요

= It is better. / Please feel better.

젓다 = to stir (liquid)

젓 + 어요 (present tense) → 저어요

= I stir. / Please stir it.

180

잇다 = to connect; to link

잇 + 었어요 (past tense) → 이었어요

= I connected (it). / I linked (it).

짓다 = to build; to compose

짓 + 었어요 (past tense) → 지었어요

= I built it. / I composed it.

Sample Sentences

잘 저으세요.

= Stir it well.

Track 57

두 개를 이었어요.

= I connected the two (objects).

이 집을 누가 지었어요?

= Who built this house?

좋은 이름을 지을 거예요.

= I am going to create a good name.

감기 다 나았어요?

= Did you recover (completely) from the cold?

Exceptions

There are some verb stems in which the "ㅅ" 받침 is regular, meaning that the ㅅ is not dropped and it stays the same.

Ex)

웃다 = to smile; to laugh

웃어요. = Smile. / I smile. / He laughs. / They laugh.

씻다 = to wash

씻을 거예요. = I am going to wash up. / I am going to wash it.

**Track
57**

벗다 = to take (clothes) off

신발을 벗어 주세요. = Please take your shoes off.

Sample Dialogue

Track 58

A: 강아지 이름이 뭐예요?

B: 코코예요.

A: 누가 지었어요?

B: 제가 지었어요.

A: *What is the name of your dog?*

B: *It is Coco.*

A: *Who named him/her?*

B: *I named him/her.*

by Learning Irregularities, Linking Verbs, Politeness Levels, and Much More

Check the answers on **p.199**

✏ Exercises for Lesson **29**

Translate the following phrases to Korean:

1. It's better / Please feel better.
  * 낫다 = to heal; to recover; to feel better

( )

2. Who built this house?
  * 짓다 = to build; to compose

( )

3. Stir it well.
  * 젓다 = to stir

( )

4. I connected the two (objects).
  * 잇다 = to connect

( )

5. Please take your shoes off.
  * 벗다 = to take off

( )

LESSON **30**

Word Builder 2

실(室)

Word Builder lessons are designed to help you understand how to more efficiently expand your vocabulary by learning/understanding some common and basic building blocks of Korean words. Many (not all) of the words and letters introduced through Word Builder lessons are based on Chinese characters, or 한자, but the meanings can differ from modern-day Chinese. Your goal, through these lessons, is to understand how words are formed and remember the keywords in Korean in order to expand your Korean vocabulary from there. You certainly do not have to memorize the Hanja characters, but if you want to, feel free!

The keyword in this lesson is 실.

The Chinese character for 실 is 室.

The word 실 is related to "room".

Sample Expressions

화장 (makeup) + 실 (room) = 화장실 (化粧室) = toilet; bathroom

* 분장 (扮裝) also means "makeup", but is specific to stage/theater makeup.
Therefore, 분장실 (扮裝室) = dressing room; backstage powder room

교 (school, teach) + 실 (room) = 교실 (教室) = classroom

연습 (practice) + 실 (room) = 연습실 (練習室) = practice room, practice place

대기 (wait) + 실 (room) = 대기실 (待機室) = waiting room

회 (meet) + 의 (discuss) + 실 (room) = 회의실 (會議室) = meeting room, conference room

병 (disease) + 실 (room) = 병실 (病室) = hospital room, patient's room

미용 (beauty treatment) + 실 (room) = 미용실 (美容室) = beauty parlor; hair salon

사 (work) + 무 (work, task) + 실 (room) = 사무실 (事務室) = office

교 (school, teach) + 무 (work) + 실 (room) = 교무실 (教務室) = teacher's office

실 (room) + 장 (head, leader) = 실장 (室長) = head of the office

실 (room) + 내 (inside) = 실내 (室內) = indoors

실 (room) + 외 (outside) = 실외 (室外) = outdoors, outside

Sample Dialogue

Track 60

A: 면접은 어디에서 봐요?

B: 회의실에서 봐요. 대기실에서 기다려 주세요.

A: 네, 알겠습니다.

A: Where do I have an interview?

B: You will have it in the meeting room. Please wait in the waiting room.

A: Okay, I will.

by *Learning Irregularities, Linking Verbs, Politeness Levels,* and *Much More*

✎ Exercises for Lesson **30**

1. The word (   ) is related to "room".

Write the following words in Korean. All given words are Sino-Korean.

2. Toilet; bathroom
    * 화장 (化粧) = make-up

(   )

3. Classroom
    * 교 (敎) = school; teach

(   )

4. Hospital room; patient's room
    * 병 (病) = disease

(   )

5. Indoors
    * 내 (內) = inside

(   )

Check the answers on **p.199**

CHUSEOK
(추석)

추석 (Chuseok) is one of the biggest national holidays in Korea along with 설날 (Lunar New Year) and 단오 / 수릿날 (Spring Festival) and is often referred to as "Korean Thanksgiving". During this 3-day holiday, Koreans travel back to their 고향 (hometown) to celebrate together, share stories, eat 맛있는 음식 (delicious food), and most importantly, to give thanks to their 조상 (ancestors).

The 3-day 추석 holiday will be observed over September 14-16 in 2016, with the actual 추석 day falling on September 15. Although Korea officially follows the Gregorian calendar, the date of 추석 is based on the 음력 (lunar calendar); a calendar based on the cycles of the lunar phase. On this calendar, 추석 is always on the 15th day of the eighth month; however, when placed on the Gregorian calendar, the date of 추석 will be different every year. For example, in 2017, 추석 is October 4, which means the 3-day holiday will be October 3 through to October 5.

Korea also has a "substitute holiday system" to give people an extra day off work . For example, when 추석 or 설날 fall on a Sunday or another public holiday, the following work day will become a non-working day. Additionally, if 어린이날 (Children's Day) falls on a Saturday, Sunday, or another public holiday, people are allowed to take off the following work day.

A little bit of history...

추석 was originally known as 한가위 (Hangawi) and still sometimes is referred to as such. Although the exact origin of 추석 is unknown, popular belief and history will tell us that 추석 originated from a month-long weaving competition between two teams during the reign of the third king (태종 무열왕) of the Silla Kingdom. The team that wove the most cloth won, and the winning team would be treated to a big feast by the losing team.

However, some scholars believe 추석 stems from the shamanistic practice of worshipping/celebrating and giving thanks to the harvest moon and ancestors. Farmers harvested crops during this time of year, and after the 추수 (harvest), would give thanks to their ancestors in a ritual of worship/thanks called 차례. By presenting their ancestors in the sky with a table of items from the new harvest, the farmers paid homage to their gracious ancestors they believe gave them a bountiful harvest so they could spend the winter months warmly and with plenty of food. They would then share their bounty and products of the first harvest with family, friends, and neighbors.

The celebration continued under the bright light of the 달 (moon) with a performance of the 강강수월래, or "circle dance", which incorporates singing, dancing, and playing instruments exclusively by the maidens of the town dressed in their most special 한복. During the day, there was also a 씨름 (Korean wrestling) competition to see who was the town's strongest man. You can still witness these traditions during present-day 추석 celebrations as well as a variety of other folk games.

Current traditions

Nowadays, there's always a mass exodus of Koreans returning to their hometown or village to join their family and to pay their respects. Highways are packed, cross-country bus and train stations are chaotic, and tickets for said buses and trains are absolutely, positively 매진 (sold out).

If you plan to travel anywhere in, out of, or around Korea during the days of 추석, it's a good idea to book your tickets WAY in advance. If this type of traveling chaos makes you uneasy, it might be best to just stay where you are and hide under a blanket until 추석 is over. Another option is, of course, to just stay where you are and enjoy the crowd-less streets and festivities in town.

On the eve of 추석, it is common for families to gather together to make one of the representative foods of the holiday, 송편 (songpyeon). These half moon-shaped rice cakes are filled with various things, such as sweet red beans, chestnuts, and sesame seeds. The making of 송편 brings everyone together to re-connect with each other and live happily in the moment. Traditionally, if the shape of your 송편 is beautifully made, it means you may have a beautiful daughter in the future.

Koreans wake up in the wee hours of the morning on the day of 추석 to perform 차례. This ceremony is not all that dissimilar from the ritual performed in days past. By dressing in traditional 한복 and setting a table with an abundance of foods - with the star of the table usually being freshly harvested rice - the family gives thanks to their ancestors. They then sit down at the table to enjoy a meal which is representative of their blessings from their ancestors.

During 추석, the family will perform 성묘. 성묘 is a noun which literally translates to "a visit to the tomb/graves of one's ancestors". When the family visits the grave site, they remove the weeds, trim plants which have grown around the grave during the summer, and offer food and drink to their ancestors. This practice is called 벌초 (Beolcho) and is considered an expression of filial piety.

Tips for surviving 추석 if you're a 외국인 (foreigner):

* Double check the operating hours of the stores and restaurants you may possibly want to visit during the holiday. They may or may not be open!
* Find places to go to which are easily accessible by subway to avoid the holiday road traffic. Subway stations will be virtually EMPTY, and you will be able to grab a seat anywhere you want to on the day of 추석.
* For the few days leading up to 추석, do not visit E-mart, Home Plus, or any grocery-like store for that matter, unless you are an adventure-seeker and enjoy getting trampled by 아줌마들 (ajummas).
* The palaces in Seoul, The Korean Folk Village, and 남산골 (Namsangol) Village have various 추석 activities, and some museums may have 추석 attractions as well!
* If you want to avoid Korea altogether during 추석, you can book a ticket well in advance to get out of the country and go sight-seeing somewhere else for the holiday.

추석 is a very special time for Korea, and if you are given the chance to experience any of the festivities or rituals, do not pass up the opportunity to engulf yourself in traditional Korean culture.

Whew! You've completely mastered Level 3!
Congratulations, and we can't wait to meet up with you again
soon for Level 4! Woohoo!

ANSWERS
for Level 3, Lessons 1 ~ 30

Answers for Level 3, Lesson 1

1. 너무

2. 너무

3. 너무 빨라요.

4. 너무 맛있어요.

5. 너무 졸려요.

Answers for Level 3, Lesson 2

1. 어제 친구를 만났고, 영화를 봤어요.

   or 어제 친구를 만나고, 영화를 봤어요.

2. 내일 영화를 볼 거고, 쇼핑하러 갈 거예요.

   or 내일 영화를 보고, 쇼핑하러 갈 거예요.

3. 만나고 or 만날 거고

4. 먹고 or 먹었고

5. 책 읽고, 공부하고, 운동했어요.

Answers for Level 3, Lesson 3

1. 앞　　　a. front

2. 위　　　d. top

3. 밑　　　e. bottom

4. 뒤　　　b. back

5. 옆　　　c. side

6. 위에서 : 소파 위에서 자고 있어요.

Answers for Level 3, Lesson 4

1. 볼까요?

2. 팔까요?

3. 올까요 : 내일 비가 올까요?

4. 우유 마실까요? 주스 마실까요?

5. 내일 (우리) 영화 볼까요?

Answers for Level 3, Lesson 5

1. -쯤, 정도, 약

2. 한 달쯤, 한 달 정도, 약 한 달

3. 언제쯤 갈 거예요?

4. 내일 몇 시쯤 만날까요?

5. 한국에서 2년쯤 살았어요. or 한국에서 2년 정도 ...

   or 한국에서 약 2년 ...

Answers for Level 3, Lesson 6

1. a. 공부할 거예요.

2. b. 저도 갈게요.

3. b. 친구들 만날 거예요.

4. 지금 어디예요? 지금 나갈게요.

5. 그래요? 다시 할게요.

Answers for Level 3, Lesson 7

1. 해서

2. 먹어서

3. 와서

4. c. -에 따라서

5. a. 예를 들어서

Answers for Level 3, Lesson 8

1. 비슷하다

2. 우리는 나이가 같아요.

3. 이거랑 이거랑 같아요?

4. 커피 같아요.

5. 그 이야기는 거짓말 같아요.

Answers for Level 3, Lesson 9

1. I think they told them. / It looks like they talked.

   b. 이야기한 것 같아요.

2. I think they are talking. / They seem to talk to each

   c. 이야기하는 것 같아요.

3. I think they will talk. / It seems like they will talk.

   a. 이야기할 것 같아요.

4. 여기 비싼 것 같아요.

5. 그런 것 같아요.

Answers for Level 3, Lesson 10

1. 전에

2. 공부하기 전에

3. 돈을 내기 전에

4. 들어오기 전에 노크하세요.

5. 사기 전에 잘 생각하세요.

Answers for Level 3, Lesson 11

1. a. 입다

2. b. 어려웠어요

3. 이거 너무 귀여워요.

4. 이 문제는 어려워요.

5. 서울은 겨울에 정말 추워요.

Answers for Level 3, Lesson 12

1. 그래도

2. 그래도

3. 비가 왔어요. 그래도

4. 어려워요. 그래도

Answers for Level 3, Lesson 13

1. 작은

2. 비싼

3. 하얀

4. 단

5. 더 큰 가방 있어요?

Answers for Level 3, Lesson 14

1. someone I like - b. 좋아하는 사람

2. someone who Minji likes - c. 민지가 좋아하는 사람

3. someone who likes Minji - a. 민지를 좋아하는 사람

4. 자주 먹는 한국 음식 있어요?

5. 요즘 좋아하는 가수는 누구예요?

Answers for Level 3, Lesson 15

1. 그러면

1-1. 그럼

2. 지금 바빠요? 그럼 언제 안 바빠요?

3. 그러면 이거는 뭐예요?

Answers for Level 3, Lesson 16

1. -아/어/여요

2. d. -(으)ㄴ

3. c. 시작하고 싶어요.

4. 같이 가요!

5. 우리 햄버거 먹어요.

Answers for Level 3, Lesson 17

1. 위해; 위해서

2. 건강을 위해서

3. 한국에 가기 위해서

4. (저는) 한국에 가기 위해서 열심히 공부했어요.

5. (저는) 건강을 위해서 매일 운동하고 있어요.

Answers for Level 3, Lesson 18

1. To have nothing but money, to only have money
   - b. 돈밖에 없다

2. To have money - c. 돈(이) 있다

3. To not have money - a. 돈(이) 없다

4. 한국인 친구는 한 명 밖에 없어요.

5. 한국어 조금밖에 못해요.

Answers for Level 3, Lesson 19

1. 편지를 받은 다음에 or 편지를 받은 후에 or
   편지를 받은 뒤에

2. 책을 읽은 다음에 or 책을 읽은 후에 or
   책을 읽은 뒤에

3. 영화 본 다음에 우리 커피 마셔요.

4. 결정한 후에 연락 주세요.

5. 이거 한 다음에 뭐 할 거예요?

Answers for Level 3, Lesson 20

1. 울어도

2. 공부해도

3. 봐도

4. 택시를 타도, 시간이 오래 걸려요.

5. 집에 가도, 밥이 없어요.

Answers for Level 3, Lesson 21

1. 내일 일요일인데, 뭐 할 거예요?

2. 어제 자고 있었는데, 한국에서 전화가 왔어요.

3. 영화 봤는데, 무서웠어요.

4. 오늘 뉴스에서 봤는데, 그거 진짜예요?

5. 이거 좋은데요!

Answers for Level 3, Lesson 22

1. 알 수도 있다

2. 만날 수도 있다

3. 작을 수도 있다

4. 저 내일 올 수도 있어요.

5. 이거 가짜일 수도 있어요.

Answers for Level 3, Lesson 23

1. 학 (學)

2. 전학 (轉學)

3. 장학금 (獎學金)

4. 수학 (數學)

5. 학년 (學年)

Answers for Level 3, Lesson 24

1. 골랐어요.

2. 뭐 골랐어요?

3. 잘랐어요.

4. 누가 케이크 잘랐어요?

5. 비행기는 빨라서 좋아요.

Answers for Level 3, Lesson 25

1. 잘 어울리네요.

2. 맞네요.

3. 여기 있네요.

4. 별로 안 춥네요.

5. 벌써 11월이네요.

Answers for Level 3, Lesson 26

1. 듣다 = to listen → 듣 + 어서 - i. 들어서

2. 걷다 = to walk → 걷 + 어요 - f. 걸어요

3. 받다 = to receive → 받 + 아서 - b. 받아서

4. 닫다 = to close → 닫 + 으면 - d. 닫으면

5. 깨닫다 = to realize → 깨닫 + 았어요 -
   h. 깨달았어요

6. 어디에서 들었어요?

Answers for Level 3, Lesson 27

1. 안녕. Hello.

2. 이거 뭐야? What is this?

3. 어제 친구 만났어. I met a friend yesterday.

4. a. True

5. b. False

Answers for Level 3, Lesson 28

1. 하자.

2. 하지 말자.

3. 이거 사자.

4. 조금만 더 기다리자.

5. 같이 가자.

Answers for Level 3, Lesson 29

1. 나아요

2. 이 집을 누가 지었어요?

3. 잘 저으세요.

4. 두 개를 이었어요.

5. 신발을 벗어 주세요.

Answers for Level 3, Lesson 30

1. 실 (室)

2. 화장실 (化粧室)

3. 교실 (敎室)

4. 병실 (病室)

5. 실내 (室內)

Notes On Using This Book

Colored Text
Colored text indicates that there is an accompanying audio file. You can download the MP3 audio files at **https://talktomeinkorean.com/audio**.

Hyphen
Some grammar points have a hyphen attached at the beginning, such as -이/가, -(으)ㄹ 거예요, -(으)려고 하다, and -은/는커녕. This means that the grammar point is dependent, so it needs to be attached to another word such as a noun, a verb, or a particle.

Parentheses
When a grammar point includes parentheses, such as -(으)ㄹ 거예요 or (이)랑, this means that the part in the parentheses can be omitted depending on the word it is attached to.

Slash
When a grammar point has a slash, such as -아/어/여서 or -은/는커녕, this means that only one of the syllables before or after the slash can be used at a time. In other words, -은/는커녕 is used as either -은커녕 or -는커녕, depending on the word it is attached to.

Descriptive Verb
In TTMIK lessons, adjectives in English are referred to as "descriptive verbs" because they can be conjugated as verbs depending on the tense.